Nelson Mandela

Other books in the Heroes and Villains series include:

Heroes and Villains

Nelson Mandela

Andy Koopmans

LUCENT BOOKS®

THOMSON

GALE

San Diego • Detroit • New York • San Francisco • Cleveland • New Haven. Conn. • Waterville. Maine • London • Munich

On cover: A beaming Nelson Mandela appears in tribal dress during his 1994 campaign to become president of South Africa.

For more information, contact
Lucent Books
27500 Drake Rd.
Farmington Hills, MI 48331-3535
Or you can visit our Internet site at http://www.gale.com

LIBRARY OF CONGRESS CATALOGING-IN-PUBLICATION DATA

Koopmans, Andy.
   Nelson Mandela / by Andy Koopmans.
      p. cm. — (Heroes and villains series)
     Includes bibliographical references (p.).
Profiles the life, career, and imprisonment of Nelson Mandela, the courageous African antiapartheid revolutionary. Also discussed is his prominence as a statesman following his release from prison.
    ISBN 1-59018-426-2
1. Mandela, Nelson, 1918– — Juvenile literature. 2. Presidents—South Africa—Biography—Juvenile literature. I. Title. II. Series.
DT 1974.K66 2004
968.06'5'092—dc22
                                         2004000381

Printed in the United States of America

Contents

Foreword

Good and evil are an ever-present feature of human history. Their presence is reflected through the ages in tales of great heroism and extraordinary villainy. Such tales provide insight into human nature, whether they involve two people or two thousand, for the essence of heroism and villainy is found in deeds rather than in numbers. It is the deeds that pique our interest and lead us to wonder what prompts a man or woman to perform such acts.

Samuel Johnson, the eminent eighteenth-century English writer, once wrote, "The two great movers of the human mind are the desire for good, and fear of evil." The pairing of desire and fear, possibly two of the strongest human emotions, helps explain the intense fascination people have with all things good and evil—and by extension, heroic and villainous.

People are attracted to the person who reaches into a raging river to pull a child from what could have been a watery grave for both, and to the person who risks his or her own life to shepherd hundreds of desperate black slaves to safety on the Underground Railroad. We wonder what qualities these heroes possess that enable them to act against self-interest, and even their own survival. We also wonder if,

under similar circumstances, we would behave as they do.

Evil, on the other hand, horrifies as well as intrigues us. Few people can look upon the drifter who mutilates and kills a neighbor or the dictator who presides over the torture and murder of thousands of his own citizens without feeling a sense of revulsion. And yet, as Joseph Conrad writes, we experience "the fascination of the abomination." How else to explain the overwhelming success of a book such as Truman Capote's *In Cold Blood*, which examines in horrifying detail a vicious and senseless murder that took place in the American heartland in the 1960s? The popularity of murder mysteries and Court TV are also evidence of the human fascination with villainy.

Most people recoil in the face of such evil. Yet most feel a deep-seated curiosity about the kind of person who could commit a terrible act. It is perhaps a reflection of our innermost fears that we wonder whether we could resist or stand up to such behavior in our presence or even if we ourselves possess the capacity to commit such terrible crimes.

The Lucent Books Heroes and Villains series capitalizes on our fascination with the perpetrators of both good and evil by introducing readers to some of history's most revered heroes and hated villains. These include heroes such as Frederick Douglass, who knew firsthand the humiliation of slavery and, at great risk to himself, publicly fought to abolish the institution of slavery in America. It also includes villains such as Adolf Hitler, who is remembered both for the devastation of Europe and for the murder of 6 million Jews and thousands of Gypsies, Slavs, and others whom Hitler deemed unworthy of life.

Each book in the Heroes and Villains series examines the life story of a hero or villain from history. Generous use of primary and secondary source quotations gives readers eyewitness views of the life and times of each individual as well as enlivens the narrative. Notes and annotated bibliographies provide stepping-stones to further research.

Father of the New South Africa

On April 27, 1994, at the age of seventy-six, Nelson Mandela cast his ballot in South Africa's presidential election. It was the first national election in which he and his fellow 14 million nonwhite South Africans were allowed to vote. It was also the election that would bring him to office as the first black president in the country's history.

The 1994 election ended the rule of the Afrikaner National Party and its institutionalized racist policies, known as apartheid, as well as over three centuries of white-minority colonial rule in South Africa. That the election ever was allowed to take place had much to do with Mandela's efforts as well as those of his colleagues in the African National Congress and other anti-apartheid groups.

Nelson Mandela has been many things in his life—a lawyer, an activist, a prisoner, and a statesman—but to the people of South Africa and many in the international community, he has also earned the right to be called a hero.

Like other Africans and nonwhites of his generation, Mandela grew up in a country where he was treated with contempt, hatred, and condescension by the ruling white minority. As Mandela writes in his autobiography, *Long Walk to Freedom*, for an African in South Africa, one's entire life was restricted by race:

> To be an African in South Africa means that one is politicized from the moment of one's birth, whether one acknowledges it or

not. An African child is born in an Africans Only hospital, taken home in an Africans Only bus, lives in an Africans Only area, and attends African Only schools, if he attends school at all.

When he grows up, he can hold Africans Only jobs, rent a house in Africans Only townships, ride Africans Only trains, and be stopped at any time of the day or night and be ordered to produce a pass, failing which he will be arrested and thrown in jail. His life is circumscribed by racist laws and regulations that cripple his growth, dim his potential, and stunt his life.[1]

Nelson Mandela spent twenty-six years as a political prisoner of the South African government for his efforts to end the racist policies of apartheid.

As an adult, instead of pursuing the relative security and prosperity within the institutionalized racism of South African society, Mandela instead chose to spend the bulk of his years—over fifty of them—tirelessly fighting against the racist government. From his first years as a young and fiery new member of the African National Congress into his ninth decade as an elderly and fiery member of that same organization, Mandela risked privation, violence, and imprisonment in the interest of common justice and democracy.

Chapter One

EARLY LESSONS

Because of his lineage and the early events of his life, Nelson Mandela experienced a youth and adolescence dramatically different from those of his peers and siblings. The mixture of his early tribal upbringing and his Western mission-school education provided him with a unique perspective of his home country. Many of these experiences formed the foundation of his later activism and leadership.

Thembu Prince

Nelson Mandela was born on July 18, 1918, in Mvezo, a small village in the district of Umtata, which was the capital of the Transkei. The Transkei was a territory in South Africa (it, like other territories, was abolished following the 1994 presidential elections) established by white European settlers and home to the Thembu. These people were a part of the Xhosa nation, a large group of tribes scattered throughout South Africa and united by a common language (Xhosa) and ancestral heritage. Mandela's father, Gadla Henry Mphakanyiswa, was a Thembu chief and part of the Madiba clan. (Throughout his life, many Xhosas and close friends called Mandela "Madiba" after his clan, a term considered a sign of respect.)

Mandela's father, Mphakanyiswa, ruled over Mvezo under the authority of the Thembu king; however, because South Africa was under British rule, his rule was subject to the approval of the British government. Although the position was still important, it had lost much of its power because of white government control.

Nonetheless, through his father, Mandela was part of royal lineage. His father's great-grandfather was King Ngubengcuka, who had ruled the Thembu in the late eighteenth and early nineteenth centuries, before Europeans owned most of the land and dominated the country. Although Mandela's father was a minor king and Mandela a minor prince, neither was heir to the throne of Ngubengcuka. African chiefs practiced polygamy, each taking several wives, and only the children of the first wife, from the "great house," were heir to the monarchy. Mandela's paternal great-great-grandmother had been Ngubengcuka's third wife, from the Ixhiba or "left-hand" house. Men from the Ixhiba house were trained to be counselors to the kings. Therefore, as a descendant of this house, Mandela's father, Mphakanyiswa, was an adviser to the Thembu king, and Mandela himself was intended to serve that role in adulthood.

This simple hut in the village of Mvezo was Mandela's childhood home. Mandela was the son of the chief of the Thembu, a South African tribe.

Mphakanyiswa had four wives, the third of whom was Mandela's mother, a woman named Nosekeni Fanny. Each of Mphakanyiswa's wives had her own homestead miles from the others, and he traveled among them. By his four wives, Mphakanyiswa sired thirteen children, four of whom were sons. Mandela was his father's youngest son and his mother's oldest child and only son. (Mandela had three younger sisters, named Baliwe, Notancu, and Makhutswana.) When Mandela was born, his father named him Rolihlahla, which, in the Xhosa language, means "troublemaker."

Boyhood in Qunu

Mandela's father was a serious and stern man and a strict disciplinarian with his children. Mandela recalls that his father also had an often troublesome and proud rebelliousness, which he passed on to his son. For instance, when Mandela was only months old, Mphakanyiswa was ordered to appear before the British magistrate regarding a legal matter; however, Mphakanyiswa refused, symbolically failing to recognize British rule over his own authority as chief. For his disobedience, Mandela's father was stripped of his chieftaincy and lost his fortune.

Following this, Mandela's mother was forced to move with her children back to her family village of Qunu to the north of Mvezo, where she would have support in raising the children.

Mphakanyiswa still visited each of his wives regularly, and although Mandela's mother and her children had to live in a less-grand style than in Mvezo, Mandela enjoyed a simple and pleasurable life in the village.

Mandela's family lived in a group of three windowless mud huts, each devoted to a purpose: cooking, sleeping, and storage. There were few men in the village because most were forced by the expense of the government's taxation to spend most of their time away from home working on faraway farms or in the mines in the Transvaal hundreds of miles away.

The women and children of the village raised corn, beans, sorghum, and pumpkins, which formed their principal diet. The work was hard, and at five years old Mandela also worked as a herd boy tending sheep and cattle in the fields. In his free time, he played and fought with other boys in the veld, or grassland. He later recalled those days as some of his happiest.

Mission-School Boy

Although his parents were illiterate and without formal education, they decided that Mandela should go to school in Qunu. Like many schools in South Africa available to Africans at the time, it was a mission school run by a Western church.

On his first day of school, his teacher gave each of the students an English name by which they would be called in school. Mandela was given the name Nelson, possibly after the famed British sea captain Lord Nelson. Along with his new English name, Mandela received a British education. As one biographer writes, the school principal at Clarkebury taught Mandela and other students that "there was no such thing as African culture, and that they, the natives, were indeed privileged to be educated by such a fine and civilized Englishman as himself."[2]

Change of Circumstance

In 1927, soon after Mandela started school, his father died. It was among his father's last wishes that Mandela continue his education, which he could not do in Qunu because of the limited resources of the village school. Because of this and because Mphakanyiswa wanted his son to have the guidance of a man he respected, he had arranged for Mandela to live in the Thembu capital, Mqhekezeweni, with the Thembu chief Jongintaba Dalindyebo.

As was tradition among the Thembu, Mandela was accepted into the household as a member of the family. He lived with the chief, Dalindyebo's wife NoEngland, and their two children, a son named Justice and a daughter, Nomafu. Mandela roomed with Justice, wore the same clothes as him, was subject to the same chores, and received the same familial affection. Justice, who was four years older

than Mandela, was athletic, handsome, and intelligent and became Mandela's brother, friend, and role model.

Church and Chieftaincy

Mandela continued his mission-school education in the Methodist school at Mqhekezeweni. After school he worked as a plowboy, a wagon guide, and a shepherd. He also did many chores around the house for the chief, running many errands and taking special pride in ironing the chief's trousers.

The major influences on Mandela at Mqhekezeweni were the church

After Mandela's father lost his chieftaincy, Mandela and his siblings moved with their mother to the village of Qunu, where they lived in a small complex of huts like this.

and the chieftaincy. With the chief and his family, Mandela attended mass every week and became a devout Methodist. Additionally, he spent many hours observing the chief during tribal meetings, which all adult male Thembus were allowed to attend.

Dalindyebo's behavior as he presided at these meetings set an example that Mandela strived to follow later in life. The chief would sit silently and listen to everyone speak. When all business and speeches had been concluded, the chief would finally speak, working to build consensus among the members. Mandela writes:

I will always remember the regent's [chief's] axiom: a leader, he said, is like a shepherd. He stays behind the flock, letting the most nimble go out ahead, whereupon the others follow, not realizing that all along they are being directed from behind.[3]

Before the White Man Came

Growing up in his mother's village of Qunu, Mandela learned of the exciting and adventurous history of his ancestors from tribal elders who nightly would gather and speak around a large fire. They often described the days before the white man came to their land. Quoted in Fatima Meer's Higher than Hope: The Authorized Biography of Nelson Mandela, *Mandela recalls these inspiring portrayals that later served as a foundation for his political philosophies.*

Then our people lived peacefully, under the democratic rule of their kings and their councilors, and moved freely and confidently up and down the country without let or hindrance. Then the country was ours. We occupied the land, the forests, the rivers; we extracted the mineral wealth beneath the soil and all the riches of this beautiful country. We set up and operated our own government, we controlled our own armies and we organized our own commerce. The elders would tell tales about the wars fought by our ancestors in defence of the fatherland, as well as acts of valour performed by generals and soldiers during those epic days....

The land, then the main means of production, belonged to the whole tribe and there was no individual ownership whatsoever. There were no classes, no rich or poor and no exploitation of man by man. All men were free and equal and this was the foundation of government....

There was much in such a society that was primitive and insecure.... But, in such a society are contained the seeds of evolutionary democracy in which none will be held in slavery or servitude, and in which poverty, want and insecurity shall be no more.

Because of these meetings, Mandela also became fascinated with African history. He learned about African heroes from all over the country from the men who visited Dalindyebo. One was Chief Zwelibhangile Joyi, an elderly sage who told Mandela how the white man had come and deliberately destroyed the African tribes, killing or conquering the people, and taking their land for the queen of England. Mandela reacted to the stories emotionally. Biographer Fatima Meer writes that Joyi's stories "laid the foundations of his historical perceptions."[4]

Western Influence

However much these stories intrigued Mandela, he was equally influenced by Western culture. At school and amidst the Westernized customs of Mqhe-kezeweni, Mandela was taught to see whites as benefactors, not oppressors.

Through his mission schooling, he also learned to speak and write English and learned the history of Africa from the European point of view.

Mandela's Western education continued as he progressed from grammar school into high school and then into

A photo of Mandela at the age of nineteen shows him dressed in a suit and tie. Mandela was deeply influenced by Western culture.

college. Chief Dalindyebo told Mandela that his destiny was to become a counselor to Justice when he one day became chief. For that, he had to be well educated. Since there were no schools beyond the grammar school at Mqhekezeweni, in 1934, when Mandela was sixteen, Dalindyebo sent him to Clarkebury Boarding Institution. The school was a Methodist-run Thembu college several hundred miles to the west, where Justice had attended a few years earlier.

College

After graduating from Clarkebury in 1937, Mandela enrolled at Healdtown, a Methodist college in Fort Beaufort, where Justice was an upperclassman. Healdtown was the largest educational establishment for Africans in South Africa. It was coeducational and provided a wide range of educational opportunities, with an emphasis on Christian and liberal arts education. Students at Healdtown were required to wear Western school uniforms, attend church, and participate in sports. Mandela adapted well to the routines of Healdtown and took up several sports, including running and boxing, both of which would remain passions of his for years to come.

After two years at Clarkebury, Mandela entered Fort Hare College to study for his bachelor's degree. He set out on a course of study that would prepare him to go to law school after graduation. The prestigious college was considered the center of higher education for blacks in South Africa. Mandela was rightfully proud to be there. As biographer Martin Meredith writes:

> Fort Hare was an educational institute for Africans of unique importance. To reach there . . . represented a great achievement. To obtain a degree from there . . . ensured personal fortune and advancement in any career then open to Africans. No other place in South Africa offered such opportunity.[5]

Politics

At Fort Hare, Mandela entered politics for the first time. A serious and hardworking student with an ambition to become an attorney, in 1940 he was nominated to the Student Representative Council, the highest student organization at the school. Shortly before the election, Mandela and his fellow nominees joined the student body in boycotting the election in protest of the poor food quality at the school.

When the boycott failed because a few students did vote, Mandela and the other elected members resigned in protest. However, a second election was held and the same handful of students voted and the same candidates were reelected. Mandela again protested but was the only council member to object to the results again. He was threatened with expulsion if he resigned.

Caught in a Lie

In late 1940 Mandela and his adopted brother Justice fled to Johannesburg to avoid the arranged marriages that Chief Dalindyebo had planned for them. In his memoir Mandela: An Illustrated Biography, *Mandela describes how he and Justice stole and lied to make their escape from Mqhekezeweni.*

We had almost no money between us, but we went to see a local trader and sold him two of [Chief Dalindyebo's] prize oxen. He paid us a very good price, and with the money we hired a car to take us to the local station where we could catch a train.

We managed to get a train to Queenstown.... But for an African to leave his magisterial district and enter another he also needed travel documents, a permit and a letter from his ... guardian—none of which we had.

Our plan was to go to the house of a relative ... and arrange the necessary documents.... We met Chief Mpondombini, a brother of the regent, who was fond of Justice and myself ... and explained that we needed travel documents from the local magistrate, claiming that we were on an errand for the regent. The Chief not only escorted us to the magistrate, but vouched for us and explained our predicament. But the magistrate said that, as a matter of courtesy, he ought to [telephone] the chief magistrate in Umtata.... As luck would have it, [Chief Dalindyebo] was just paying a call on the chief magistrate ... and was in his very office. When [Chief Dalindyebo] heard what we were requesting, he exploded, and ordered the magistrate to arrest us.... I immediately rose to our defence. We had told him lies, that was true. But we had committed no offence and violated no laws. ... The magistrate backed down, but told us to leave his office and never darken his door again.

Justice remembered he had a friend ... who was working in the office of a white attorney. We went to see him and explained our situation; he told us that the mother of the attorney was driving into Johannesburg and would give us a ride if we paid a fee of 15 [pounds]. This was a vast sum, which virtually depleted our savings, but we had no choice. We [accepted and] decided to risk getting the correct travel documents once we were in Johannesburg.

Mandela was not sure what he should do. His education was very important to him. He later recalled his quandary:

> Even though I thought what I was doing was morally right, I was still uncertain as to whether it was the correct course. Was I sabotaging my academic career over an abstract moral principle that mattered very little? . . . I had taken a stand, and I did not want to appear to be a fraud in the eyes of my fellow students. At the same time, I did not want to throw away my career at Fort Hare.[6]

Mandela decided to resign, and as promised, he was expelled. He packed his things and returned to Mqhekezeweni to face the certain disappointment of Chief Dalindyebo.

Indeed, Dalindyebo was angry and chastised Mandela for jeopardizing his future. However, after a few days, it seemed that the chief's wrath had subsided and Mandela fell back into his routines at the royal palace. Justice had also returned to Mqhekezeweni, and they were glad to see each other.

Runaway

A few weeks after Mandela's return, the chief told him and Justice that he was in ill health and feared he was going to die soon. He told them that he had arranged to settle his affairs

before his death, including the matter of arranging marriages for the two young men. He had already selected their brides and paid the dowry to the fathers of the girls.

Justice and Mandela were stunned. They did not want their marriages arranged for them; however, they did not argue with the chief as it was not allowed. Miserable, and feeling he had no other choice, Mandela decided to run away to Johannesburg, the capital city of South Africa. Justice agreed to leave with him.

The two had no money, so one morning when the chief was away on business, they stole two of Dalindyebo's prized oxen and sold them to a local trader to gain enough money for train fare. However, their plot was foiled temporarily. Anticipating they might run away, the chief had sent pictures of the boys to the train station with the instructions not to let them board any train. They did not give up, however, and after a series of setbacks the two were able to arrange a ride in a private vehicle to Johannesburg. As biographer Meredith writes, within only a few weeks, Mandela's fortunes had greatly changed:

> One minute he was part of an African elite, attending the most advanced educational institute for Africans in South Africa, assured of prosperity and prestige. . . . A few weeks later . . . he was bound, virtually penniless, for a city renowned for its harsh and violent character.[7]

As Mandela approached Johannesburg, however, he thought of the romantic appeal of the great city he had never seen before but heard about all his life. It was almost ten in the evening when they reached the outskirts. Mandela saw the glimmer of the enormous maze of lights in the distance—an almost miraculous sight in a country where electric light was still a luxury. Johannesburg was known as "the City of Gold," and he approached it not knowing what fortune or adventure lay ahead.

Chapter Two

A Political Awakening

Mandela arrived in Johannesburg in 1941, unaware that his life there would so dramatically shape his future. His intention was to find employment, complete his bachelor's degree, and enter the small black elite of South Africa's Westernized, educated blacks. However, within months he met people and went through experiences in Johannesburg that awoke in him a desire to change the harsh oppression under which blacks lived in his country. He was inspired to enter the political struggle against the racist policies of the white South African government.

Johannesburg

Johannesburg was known as "the City of Gold" because it had been built at the center of the richest gold mine ever discovered, a forty-mile-long reef along an outcropping of rock called the Witwatersrand. After the discovery of gold in 1886, Johannesburg drew tens of thousands of people seeking their fortune in mining. By 1941, when Mandela and Justice arrived, the population of the city exceeded 250,000 and was growing steadily. Many who came to the city were migrant African workers—exclusively men—who worked in the mines and lived in cramped quarters in mine barracks. Johannesburg also had a large resident African population segregated to slums within the city or townships outside the city where living conditions were harsh. The city was also economically segregated; many facilities were not open to blacks and certain skilled jobs legally restricted Africans.

Upon his arrival in the bustling city, Mandela was optimistic and excited. All of his life he had heard people talk about Johannesburg, telling tales that glorified the gold mines and made a miner's life sound like one of the greatest and most respectable pursuits. Months prior to their running away, Chief Dalindyebo had written the mine headman at one of the largest mines, Crown Mines, to arrange a future position for Justice as a clerk in the office. The position was one of the most respectable a young African man could hold. Justice anticipated getting both himself and Mandela good jobs.

First Job

At first, things went well for the pair. Because of the chief's prior arrangements, both men were able to secure work immediately. Justice clerked while Mandela was made a night watchman with the possibility of a later promotion to clerk. Meanwhile, many of the Thembu men at the mines treated Justice with reverence because of his royal lineage. They gave him numerous gifts, which he shared with Mandela.

Their good fortune did not last long, however. One of the mine workers discovered that they had run away from the chief and reported this to the headman,

Most Africans in Johannesburg worked in the gold mines. As a young man, Mandela believed that a job in the mines was prestigious and respectable.

who in turn notified Dalindyebo. The chief sent a terse telegram insisting that Justice and Mandela be sent home immediately. Enraged that he had been duped into giving jobs to runaways, the headman fired Justice and Mandela and kicked them out of the barracks.

Mandela was humbled and upset by the experience. He also had no idea of what to do. "Our fortunes were now reversed. We were without jobs, without prospects, and without a place to stay,"[8] he later recalled.

Meeting Walter Sisulu

Through his father's connections, Justice was able to find a place to live, and Mandela arranged to temporarily stay with a cousin. Learning of Mandela's ambition to become a lawyer, his cousin introduced him to an influential African man named Walter Sisulu, who agreed to help Mandela find work.

Sisulu was six years older than Mandela and worked as a real estate agent who specialized in selling property to Africans. He was also a local community leader and a member of the African National Congress (ANC), an organization started in 1912 to help protect the rights of Africans.

Mandela and Sisulu became fast friends. Sisulu remembered Mandela as "a bright young man with high ideals,"[9] and Mandela was impressed with Sisulu and surprised that he had never graduated high school. Mandela recalls, "I had been taught that to have

a BA [bachelor's degree] meant to be a leader, and to be a leader one needed a BA. But in Johannesburg I found that many of the most outstanding leaders had never been to university at all."[10]

Sisulu arranged for a place for Mandela to stay in Alexandra, a black township outside Johannesburg. He also set up an interview for Mandela to work as a clerk in a white law firm in the city and even offered to help Mandela pay to finish his bachelor's degree by correspondence course.

Mandela gratefully accepted Sisulu's help. He rented a tiny tin-roofed shack at the back of another family's house. The shack had no electricity or running water, but Mandela did not mind. "It was a place of my own," he recalls, "and I was happy to have it."[11]

Law Clerk

As Sisulu promised, he arranged for Mandela to interview for a clerk's position at one of Johannesburg's largest white law firms, Witkin, Sidelsky, and Eidelman. The firm was Jewish-owned, and the partners in the firm were pleasant and less racist in their attitudes toward blacks than many other whites. The firm handled business for both blacks and whites, which was unusual. Equally unusual was that Lazar Sidelsky, one of the partners, agreed to hire Mandela, a black man.

Mandela (left) and African National Congress member Walter Sisulu converse in prison. The two men became close after their first meeting in Johannesburg in 1941.

In his thirties and among the more liberal whites in the city, Sidelsky was a man whom Mandela came to respect and like very much. Sidelsky donated one of his old suits to Mandela to wear at the office and consistently encouraged Mandela to become a successful attorney to serve as a model of achievement for other Africans.

Mandela was very happy to get the job, not only for the money but also because it was one step farther on the path to becoming an attorney. Beyond law school and professional exams to become an attorney in South Africa, one had to undergo several years of apprenticeship at a law firm—a process known as "serving articles." The position would

A Sobering Sight

Like many rural African boys, Mandela had grown up on tales about Johannesburg, renowned as "the City of Gold" due to its location on the richest gold deposits ever discovered. However, as Mandela describes in Long Walk to Freedom, *upon his arrival at Crown Mines, he was shocked and dismayed at the conditions under which the nation's white wealth was acquired.*

There is nothing magical about a gold mine. Barren and pockmarked, all dirt and no trees, fenced in all sides, a gold mine resembles a war-torn battlefield. The noise was harsh and ubiquitous: the rasp of shaft-lifts, the jangling power drills, the distant rumble of dynamite, the barked orders. Everywhere I looked I saw black men in dusty overalls looking tired and bent. They lived on the grounds in bleak, single-sex barracks that contained hundreds of concrete bunks separated from each other by only a few inches.

Gold mining . . . was costly because the ore was low grade and deep under the earth. Only the presence of cheap labor in the form of thousands of Africans working long hours for little pay with no rights made gold mining profitable for the mining houses—white owned companies that became wealthy beyond the dreams of Croesus [an ancient Lydian king renowned for his wealth] on the backs of the African people. I had never seen such great machines, such methodological organization, and such backbreaking work. It was my first sight of South African capitalism at work.

allow him to eventually become an "articled clerk" and then an attorney.

First, however, Mandela had to complete his bachelor's degree. To that end, he entered the University of South Africa as a part-time student, studying by correspondence with Fort Hare. He kept a rigorous schedule of full-time work at the law firm and part-time study in the evenings, working by candlelight in his tin-roofed shack.

Mandela's salary was barely enough to support himself and required him to sacrifice and economize. He later recalled, "I wasn't earning the monthly wage of two pounds and out of this amount I had to pay the monthly rent . . . plus bus fare . . . to town and back. It was hard going."[12] He often walked nine miles into the city to his job to save the money it cost to ride the bus, and his only hot meal of the week came when he was allowed to share

Sunday dinner with his landlord's family.

Office Politics

Working at the law firm, Mandela made a new acquaintance who first inspired his interest in African politics. He shared an office with the only other African employee in the firm, a man named Gaur Radebe. Radebe was ten years older than Mandela and worked as a clerk, interpreter, and messenger. Mandela soon learned that Radebe was a prominent member of the ANC and the Communist Party (CP), both of which were involved in the struggle for nonwhite rights in South Africa. Like Sisulu, Radebe did not have a bachelor's degree but seemed better educated than most of Mandela's college acquaintances.

Mandela's boss, Sidelsky, respected Radebe and Walter Sisulu but counseled Mandela not to become involved in politics and to avoid the men outside of work. However, Mandela met another CP member at the firm, an articled clerk named Nat Bregman who became Mandela's first white friend. Mandela and Bregman spent time together outside of work, and Bregman encouraged Mandela to learn about communism.

Although Mandela liked Bregman, Radebe, and Sisulu, at first he was not interested in getting involved in politics because his studies and his job required so much time that he felt he had little

energy for anything else. Nonetheless, Bregman took him to parties with Communists where Mandela came in contact with people of all the South African races—whites, Africans, Indians, and coloreds (the South African government's term for descendants of aboriginal Hottentots)—mingling together as if color did not matter. It impressed him, but not enough to put aside misgivings about communism, which, according to biographer Mary Benson, came from his Methodist upbringing. She writes, "His religious upbringing had taught him that communists were anti-Christ."[13]

Meeting with the Chief

Although many of Mandela's childhood beliefs influenced him, in late 1941 he realized how much he had changed in the months since his arrival in Johannesburg. Chief Dalindyebo had come to the city on business, and Mandela was apprehensive about meeting with him because it was the first time the two had seen each other since Mandela had run away. The visit was surprisingly cordial and pleasant, and the chief did not mention the arranged marriage or Mandela's running away. However, Mandela had to tell the chief that his life goals had changed. He now wanted to complete his education, pursue his law degree in Johannesburg, and stay in the city to become an attorney rather than return to Mqhekezeweni as a counselor to Justice. The chief did not try to dissuade Mandela, and they parted on good terms. Being released from his duties to the royal family made Mandela feel free.

Six months later, Mandela and Justice learned of the chief's death through the newspaper. A telegram notifying Justice of the chief's death had been lost. The two left for the Transkei to attend the funeral, but they arrived a day too late. Mandela felt disappointment and some guilt for having deserted the chief.

Justice took over duties as chief and stayed behind in Mqhekezeweni, and after a week of mourning and visiting with old friends, Mandela returned alone to Johannesburg. During the journey he reflected on how much he had changed. He later wrote:

> There is nothing like returning to a place that remains unchanged, to find the ways in which you yourself have altered. . . . I realized that my own outlook and world-views had evolved. . . . I no longer saw my future bound up with Thembuland and the Transkei. . . . I looked back on that young man who had left Mqhekezeweni as a naive and parochial fellow who had seen little of the world.[14]

A Radical Education

In 1943, a year after Chief Dalinyebo's death, Mandela completed his bache-lor's degree and enrolled as a part-time law student at Witwatersrand University in Johannesburg. He continued to work full time at the law firm. He also moved in with Walter Sisulu in Orlando West, another township outside Johannesburg.

At Witwatersrand University— known as "Wits"—Mandela was surrounded for the first time by an interracial student body. On campus there was no segregation, and he met many African nationalists, liberals, Indians, and Communists. Several of Mandela's Indian and white college acquaintances would become lifelong friends and vital allies in his later political life.

Equally important was the education Mandela received outside of college from his politically active friends, particularly Sisulu and Radebe. Despite Sidelsky's warnings, Mandela spent many hours conversing with the men, intrigued by what they had to say about the situation in South Africa. Month by month, Mandela's awareness of the dire poverty and harsh conditions in which he and other Africans lived in grew, and he became drawn to political activism.

Radebe emphasized the importance of the African National Congress as a political force and gave Mandela an in-depth informal education, suggesting books to read, introducing him to other activists, and taking him to meetings. In this way, Mandela learned about the African political history that the European schools had failed to teach him.

The Birth of a Freedom Fighter

With Radebe, Mandela attended his first political march in 1943 to protest an increase in city bus fares. It was a large protest, with twenty thousand people marching and boycotting the bus company. Participating deeply affected Mandela. He later said:

> This campaign had a great effect on me. In a small way, I had departed from my role as an observer to

Office Diplomacy

At Witkin, Sidelsky, and Eidelman, Mandela was one of two Africans employed at the otherwise all-white firm. In his autobiography, Long Walk to Freedom, *Mandela recalls an awkward moment on his first day in which he was forced to make a decision whether to offend his other black coworker or a white secretary.*

That first morning at the firm, a pleasant young white secretary, Miss Lieberman, took me aside and said, "Nelson, we have no color bar here at the law firm." She explained that at midmorning, the tea-man arrived in the front parlor with tea on a tray and a number of cups. "In honor of your arrival, we have purchased two new cups for you and Gaur [the other black clerk]," she said. . . . "I will call you when tea comes, and then you can take your tea in the new cups." . . . [I] knew that the "two new cups" she was so careful to mention were evidence of the color bar that she said did not exist. The secretaries might share tea with two Africans, but not the cups with which to drink it.

When I told Gaur . . . he said "at teatime, don't worry about anything. Just do as I do." At eleven o'clock, Miss Lieberman informed us that tea had arrived. In front of the secretaries and some other members of the firm, Gaur went over to the tea tray and ostentatiously ignored the two new cups, selecting instead one of the old ones. . . . The secretaries stared at Gaur and then Gaur nodded to me, as if to say, "It is your turn, Nelson." . . .

I neither wanted to offend the secretaries nor alienate my new colleague, so. . . . I declined to have any tea at all. . . . I saw the middle path as the best and most reasonable one. Thereafter, at teatime, I would go to the small kitchen in the office and take my tea there in solitude.

South African policemen check the passes of two native men. The South African government used the pass system to keep black Africans under control.

become a participant. I found that to march with one's people was exhilarating and inspiring. But I was also impressed by the boycott's effectiveness: after nine days, during which the buses ran empty, the company returned the fare to fourpence.[15]

Although there were several key events such as the bus boycott that affected his political outlook, in his autobiography, *Long Walk to Freedom*, Mandela says that it was the cumulative effect of many factors that led him to become an activist:

I cannot pinpoint a moment when I became politicized, when I knew that I would spend my life in the liberation struggle. . . . I had no epiphany, no singular revelation, no moment of truth, but a steady accumulation of a thousand slights, a thousand indignities, a thousand unremembered moments, produced in me an anger, a rebelliousness, a desire to fight the system that imprisoned my people. There was no particular day on which I said, From henceforth I will devote myself to the liberation of my people; instead, I simply found myself doing so, and could not do otherwise.[16]

African Nationalist

For Mandela, one of the most intriguing and inspiring political ideologies was African nationalism. The central idea of African nationalism was that, as the native race in South Africa, Africans could and should be allowed to run the country themselves. Many African nationalists believed that there was no place in the country's leadership for non-Africans. Some even believed that other races should be made to leave the country. Mandela's personal friendships with whites, coloreds, and Indians conflicted with these ideas, and the contradictions in his own beliefs made him uncertain and confused.

Nonetheless, Mandela gravitated toward the movement, particularly after meeting Anton Lembede at an ANC meeting. Lembede was one of the most influential black leaders in

Pass Laws

In his book Nelson Mandela: A Biography, *biographer Martin Meredith describes the South African pass system, one of the longest-standing tools the government implemented to control and oppress African adults.*

The official government attitude towards South Africa's black urban population was based on the commission of inquiry ... published in 1922, which asserted that "natives—men, women and children—should be permitted within municipal areas in so far and for so long as their presence is demanded by the wants of the white population" and "should depart therefrom when they ceased to minister to the needs of the white man." The towns were regarded essentially as white preserves; Africans living there were treated as "temporary sojourners," a convenient reservoir of labour for use when required, but whose real homes were in rural reserves. Hence there was no need for the authorities to make anything more than the minimum provisions [for basic necessities like shelter] for them. To ensure this policy worked, a system of pass laws was employed. African men were required to carry passes recording permission to work and live in an urban area. They needed passes for travel, for taxes, for curfews, and these were demanded for inspection by police. Mass police raids in the locations were regularly organized to ensure that the pass laws ... were being enforced, and ... the methods used were often violent.

the country, an ardent African nationalist who believed that Africa should be taken back by blacks. According to Lembede, "Africa is a black man's country. Africans are the natives of Africa and they have inhabited Africa, their Motherland from times immemorial. Africa belongs to them."[17]

Lembede warned that the whites in South Africa were trying to create an elite class of Europeanized blacks who would allow a Western-style form of government to dominate them and keep them passive. This idea made Mandela examine his own life:

African gold miners lived in dire poverty under apartheid. Mandela was shocked to witness their living and working conditions.

Lembede's views struck a chord in me. . . . I was already on my way to being drawn into the black elite that Britain sought to create in Africa. That is what everyone from the regent to Mr. Sidelsky had wanted for me. But it was an illusion. Like Lembede, I came to see the antidote as militant African nationalism.[18]

The African National Congress

With the encouragement of his ANC friends, Mandela joined the organization in 1943. Soon afterward, he helped Lembede, Sisulu, and others establish the ANC Youth League to meet the needs of the influx of young activists who believed the ANC should be more militant in its actions against the white-minority government. The ANC Youth League intended to radicalize the entire organization.

At the annual ANC conference in December 1943, Lembede and his followers officially proposed the creation of the Youth League. They also said that they were against working with non-African organizations such as the Indian Congress or Communist Party. The Youth League's manifesto read: "We believe that the national liberation of Africans will be achieved by the Africans themselves."[19]

Although the proposal for the Youth League was opposed by many of the more conservative older members, the league was voted in easily. Lembede was

Mandela's friend Oliver Tambo was the first secretary-general of the ANC Youth League.

its first president, Sisulu was the treasurer, and Mandela's old Fort Hare friend Oliver Tambo became secretary-general. Mandela, the political novice of the group, was elected as a member of the executive committee, which would help decide the league's policy and direction.

In the few years from his arrival in Johannesburg, Mandela's life had been transformed by his political awakening. At the time he was unaware of how significant the ANC would become to his life and of how consuming the struggle for racial equality would be.

Chapter Three

Learning to Lead

In the mid-1940s and early 1950s, Mandela became more committed to the newly galvanized ANC as the South African government grew increasingly oppressive. In these years, Mandela also began a family and continued to work toward his aspirations of becoming an attorney. Meanwhile, he rose through the ranks of the ANC and learned important lessons in leadership. His increasing commitment to the struggle against apartheid required him to work almost constantly to meet his obligations to family, job, and the ANC.

Family Life

Within the first months of his involvement with the ANC, Mandela also married and started a family. Sisulu introduced him to an old family friend, a nurse named Evelyn Ntoko Mase who came from a village not far from where Mandela was born. Mase later recalled that she and Mandela were attracted to each other immediately. "I think I loved him the first time I saw him," she says. "Within days of our first meeting, we were going steady, and within months he proposed. . . . Everyone we knew said that we made a very good couple."[20]

The couple dated for a short time and were married in the Native Commissioner's Court in Johannesburg in 1944. They had no money for a honeymoon because Mandela was working only part time at the law office while he studied for his law exams and was making a small salary.

Overpopulation in the townships made renting a house impossible, so they stayed with relatives until the birth of their first child, a son they named Thembi, in 1945. At that time, the government assigned them a house in the Orlando West township on the outskirts of Johannesburg. In the next few years, the couple had three more children, but only two survived past infancy—a second son named Makgatho, born in 1950, and a daughter named Makaziwe in 1954.

Mandela enjoyed being a family man although he had little time for it. His commitment to work, study, and the ANC afforded him little time to experience the simple pleasures of home life. Mandela's friend Oliver Tambo remembers that, for Mandela and himself, as for many others in the ANC, politics did not allow for much leisure or family life. "We were never really young," he says. "There were no

Nelson and his first wife Evelyn Mase were married in Johannesburg in 1944. Their first child Thembi was born in 1945.

The Apartheid Platform

In his autobiography, Long Walk to Freedom, *Mandela discusses the platform of apartheid on which the Boer-dominated Nationalist Party's philosophy and actions were based and which institutionalized the already existing racism against nonwhites in South Africa.*

The Nationalist Party's campaign centered around . . . the black danger, and they fought the election on the twin slogans of . . . The nigger in his place and . . . The coolies out of the country—*coolies* being the Afrikaner's derogatory term for Indians.

The Nationalists . . . were a party animated by bitterness . . . toward the African, who the Nationalists believed was threatening the prosperity and purity of Afrikaner culture. . . . [Nationalist Party leader Daniel] Malan's platform was known as apartheid. *Apartheid* was a new term but an old idea. It literally means "apartness" and it represented the codification in one oppressive system of all the laws and regulations that had kept Africans in an inferior position to whites for centuries. . . . The often haphazard segregation of the past three hundred years was to be consolidated into a monolithic system that was diabolical in its detail, inescapable in its reach, and overwhelming in its power. The premise of apartheid was that whites were superior to Africans, Coloureds, and Indians, and the function of it was to entrench white supremacy forever.

Apartheid policies sanctioned strict segregation at all public facilities. Even the entrance to the Johannesburg zoo was segregated.

dances, hardly a night at the cinema, but [there were] meetings, discussions, every night, every weekend."[21]

Deeper Commitment

The time and commitment activism required of Mandela grew as the events of the mid-to-late 1940s drew the ANC into unprecedented opposition to the South African government. In these years in South Africa, the end of World War II brought Mandela and other South Africans hope that segregation would be alleviated and the right to vote in national elections would be awarded to the black population. However, the government struggled to maintain the status quo of white wealth and cheap black labor under an influx of investment in South African industry. According to biographer Mary Benson, "The war, in opening the country to greater industrialization and foreign investment, had reinforced the wealth and power of the whites."[22]

In December 1945 Mandela attended the annual ANC conference, where the organization adopted a position demanding universal voting rights and the end to the color bar that restricted certain skilled jobs to whites. This open challenge to the government's power, a move championed by Mandela and other ANC Youth League members, signaled a new politicization for the ANC.

Common Ground

Under the newly politicized ANC Youth League and Anton Lembede, Mandela fought for the rights of blacks with little concern for the rights of other minority races and political groups. However, in 1946 and 1947, events transpired that began to shift the beliefs of many in the ANC.

In 1946 the Communist Party organized the largest miners strike in South African history. Pressing for higher wages, over seventy thousand miners—approximately a quarter of the African labor force in South Africa—went on strike, shutting down or disrupting production at nineteen of the country's mines. The military was sent in to end the strike, and in the process, nine people were killed and over twelve hundred were injured.

Later that year the Indian activist community led a mass campaign of nonviolent disobedience against new oppressive government laws. Indians purposefully broke the new laws in protest and voluntarily went to prison, serving as examples of the government's injustice.

These two events impressed many ANC members, and the organization leaders thought that collaboration with non-African groups would be a good strategic move. However, Mandela and others affiliated with Lembede opposed such action because they feared non-African influence would harm the ANC. As biographer Martin Meredith writes, "[Lembede and Mandela were] adamant about the need for African leadership and African control. Lembede's Africanism was essentially a philosophy of racial exclusivity."[23]

Joining Forces

However, in 1947 the ANC Youth League was thrown into chaos and mourning when Lembede suddenly died from a stomach disorder. He was succeeded by A.P. Mda, a more moderate African nationalist. Soon afterward, despite the opposition of Mandela's and Lembede's close associates, leaders of the ANC and two Indian rights groups and a colored group signed a pact to join forces against the white government. Mandela later described the pact as an important step in creating a foundation of concerted action amongst the non-white races, but at the time he was infuriated with the ANC leadership's actions.

In December of that year, in addition to his position in the ANC Youth League, Mandela was elected to the regional Executive Committee of the Transvaal ANC. As his first act on the committee, he voiced his adamant opposition to the multiparty pact and additionally opposed the first joint campaigns organized under it. He later admitted with regret that he opposed the campaigns only because the ANC was not clearly the leader in the actions.

Mandela also opposed the alliance because he feared that non-African organizations would take control of the ANC. Despite his close, personal friendships with Communists and Indians and his respect for the success of the strikes and protests led by the CP and Indians in the mid-1940s, his intolerance and fear led him to act against activists from other parties. He would disrupt their meetings, tear up signs, and even take the microphone away from speakers giving speeches.

The 1948 Election

While Mandela and other staunch Africanists fought against the intrusion of others into the ANC, South Africa's 1948 national election took place almost unnoticed by Mandela and his colleagues. Only whites could participate in South African elections, and most minorities believed that one white leader was as bad as the next. However, on the morning that the election results were announced, many, including Mandela, were dismayed and shocked to learn that the Nationalist Party had won. Formed primarily of conservative Boers (descendants of Dutch Afrikaners who had fought to keep slavery in South Africa after the British had abolished it in the nineteenth century), the party was led by Daniel Malan. The party had won the election on the platform known as apartheid—a new term that meant literally "apartness" and, as Mandela writes, represented the codification in one oppressive system of all the laws and regulations that had kept Africans in an inferior position to whites for centuries. . . . The often haphazard segregation of the past three hundred years was to be consolidated in to a monolithic system that was diabolical in its detail, inescapable in its reach, and overwhelming in its power.[24]

Daniel Malan, the leader of the Nationalist Party, won the 1948 election and implemented policies of apartheid.

Indeed, within weeks of coming to power, Malan began to implement the program of apartheid in South Africa by instituting several laws that further reduced the rights of nonwhites. One law abolished the right of coloreds to representation in Parliament, another abolished mixed marriages, and the Population Registration Act, considered the most insidious, legally classified every South African by race, making color the most important legal characteristic of each individual.

The Program of Action

In response to the new laws, the ANC Youth League pressed for the ANC to adopt a campaign known as the Program of Action, which consisted of boycotts, strikes, stay-at-home strikes (in which people would protest by not going to work and remaining in their homes), passive resistance, protest demonstrations, and other mass actions. Under South African law, all of these acts were illegal; however, Mandela and the rest of the Youth League membership were prepared for the risk.

However, the national ANC president, Alfred Xuma, strongly opposed the Program of Action. He was a doctor with a prosperous career and did not want to see it ruined by going to prison.

Mandela and his colleagues tried to persuade Xuma to accept their plan. Finally, they went to his house and gave him an ultimatum: either he supported the Program of Action or he would lose the support of the Youth League, whose numbers and influence in the organization were significant. Xuma refused the ultimatum and threw Mandela and the others out of his home. At the 1948 annual conference, the Youth League successfully deposed Xuma, bringing in J.S. Moroka, who backed the Program of Action. Additionally, Walter Sisulu was elected secretary-general of the ANC, and Oliver Tambo was elected to the National Executive Committee. Mandela himself was elected to the National Executive Committee. Mandela was inspired by the new younger leadership in place in the ANC:

This was a departure from the days of decorous protest, and many of the old stalwarts of the ANC were to fade away in this new era of greater militancy. Youth League members had now graduated to the senior organization. We had now guided the ANC to a more radical and revolutionary path.[25]

The 1950 National Protest

Although Mandela remained suspicious of non-African influence on the ANC, the first mass action led by the newly radicalized ANC began to shift his views. In March 1950 a multiparty convention called for a one-day general strike for the first of May in protest of government policies. Mandela opposed the strike, breaking up meetings, speaking against organizers, and generally attempting to disrupt the process. However, when it seemed inevitable that the strike would happen, he chose to participate in the protest marches.

The government responded to the strike by sending two thousand armed police out to stop protest marches, and Mandela was among many attacked and arrested. Mandela was deeply affected by his first violent run-in with police and was also impressed by the participation of the Indian organizations. He congratulated the groups personally and began to understand the importance of unifying all opposition groups together.

A Day of Protest

Following the attacks by police—the event became known as the May Day Slaughter—outcry and protest arose all over the country; however, the government responded by further restricting the rights of dissidents, particularly Communists, whom the government saw as the greatest threat and the leader behind the strike. The government introduced the Suppression of Communism Act of 1950, which outlawed the Communist Party of South Africa and made it a crime punishable by ten years in prison to be a member of the party.

Apartheid Laws (1949–1959)

Within the first decade of coming to power, the Nationalist Party instituted the bulk of its race-based legislation, known as the apartheid laws. This was an effort to economically and socially segregate Africans and other nonwhites. Appearing below are some of the apartheid laws.

The Prohibition of Mixed Marriages Act (1949) and Immortality Act (1950) made marriage and sexual relations illegal across the color line.

The Population Registration Act (1950) designated the racial category of every person in the country: white, Bantu (the government term for Africans), Indian, or colored (government term for nonwhites who were not African or Indian).

The Group Areas Act (1950). It restricted nonwhite racial groups' ownership of land, occupation of premises, and trade to separate areas.

Separate Representation of Voters Act (1951) reduced coloreds' voting power by removing them from the general voters' roster.

Bantu Authorities Act (1951) abolished the Natives Representative Council, the one forum of national representation for Africans, and replaced it with a hierarchical system of tribal chiefs appointed by the government.

Criminal Laws Amendment Act (1953) authorized corporeal punishment for defiers of the government.

Public Safety Act (1953) empowered the government to declare martial law and detain people without charging them with a crime.

The Reservation of Separate Amenities Act (1953) legalized separate and unequal public facilities for nonwhites.

The Bantu Education Act (1953) required all church and mission schools to turn control of their schools over to the government.

The Native Resettlement Act, also called the Western Areas Removal Act (1954), removed Africans from the townships of Sophiatown, Martindale, and Newclare to make way for the construction of white suburbs.

The Extension of University Education Act (1959) prohibited the established universities to accept a black student except with special permission from a cabinet minister.

While Parliament considered the Suppression of Communism Act, Mandela spoke before an emergency meeting of the National Executive Committee of the ANC. He spoke out against the law, saying that although it was overtly directed against the Communist Party, it was an attack on opposition in general. He said at the time, "The Bill is a further example of the determination of the white people of this country to keep the African in permanent subordination."[26]

At this meeting, the ANC planned a national day of protest and work stoppage for June 26, 1950. Flyers called for all races to participate. Mandela not only accepted the multiracial makeup of the protest but also led it, traveling all over the country to raise awareness and support. Although the protest was hastily conceived and disorganized, it was the ANC's first national campaign and it was a moderate success, with most city workers striking and most black-owned businesses not operating.

The Defiance Campaign

The next major protest was led by Mandela, who was elected Youth League president in December 1950. He worked with Walter Sisulu to organize a multiracial mass campaign of protest and civil disobedience against the apartheid laws. Known as the Defiance Campaign, the action was planned to begin April 6, 1952, the three-hundredth anniversary of the landing of Dutch explorer Jan van Riebeeck at the Cape of Good Hope in 1652, celebrated by white South Africans as the founding of their country. Meanwhile, Africans traditionally marked the date as the beginning of their enslavement.

Mandela drafted a letter to Prime Minister Malan advising him that if the government did not repeal its repressive apartheid laws by February 29, 1952, the Defiance Campaign would be launched. Malan responded that the government would not repeal the laws; further, he warned that the government would retaliate against any disturbance.

Mandela and his colleagues modeled the Defiance Campaign on the examples of passive resistance and nonviolence used by Mohandas Gandhi's followers in the struggle for Indian independence from Britain in the years following World War II. As planned, the Defiance Campaign would occur in two stages: In the first, a small number of volunteers would break selected laws in a small number of urban areas—for instance, entering whites-only facilities. They would be arrested with minimal disturbance. In the second stage, mass defiance would occur, accompanied by strikes all over South Africa.

In the first days of the Defiance Campaign, more than 250 volunteers around the country violated various apartheid laws and were imprisoned. Then, over the next five months, over

Mandela was elected ANC Youth League president in 1950. He and Sisulu immediately organized a massive protest campaign known as the Defiance Campaign.

8,500 participated. Men and women from all professions took part in the strike—teachers, doctors, factory workers, ministers, students, and lawyers. Many risked losing lucrative careers, and many put themselves in political danger for the cause. The protests were all nonviolent and seemed effective.

The government, desperate to end the campaign, decided to strike at the movement. In the Eastern Cape, where there was a long history of black and white confrontation, the government gave the ANC special permission to hold a mass prayer meeting in October. At the meeting, the military moved in and attacked the people gathered, killing eight Africans and injuring dozens. Infuriated, the mob fought back. As Fatima Meer describes:

[The mob attacked] all symbols of white power that they encountered. Two whites were killed, one of them a nun whose body was found mutilated. The violence spread to Port Elizabeth and Kimberley. The ANC was shocked and confused. It did not know how to handle violence as it was committed to non-violence.[27]

A New Era of Resistance

The 1952 Defiance Campaign, orchestrated by Mandela, then president of the ANC (Transvaal branch), was a countrywide protest in which thousands of people voluntarily violated apartheid laws and went to jail. The following excerpt from Mandela's September 1953 speech entitled "No Easy Walk to Freedom" (anthologized in a collection of Mandela's speeches and writings called The Struggle Is My Life) *was presented to the ANC (Transvaal) Conference in his absence since he was banned. In it, he celebrates the success of the campaign and declares that the people of South Africa would no longer passively abide by the government's oppressive acts.*

The intensification of repression and the extensive use of the bans are designed to immobilise every active worker and to check the national liberation movement. But gone forever are the days when harsh and wicked laws provided the oppressors with years of peace and quiet. The racial policies of the Government have pricked the conscience of all men of good will and have aroused their deepest indignation. The feelings of the oppressed people have never been more bitter. If the ruling circles seek to maintain their position by such inhuman methods then a clash between the forces of freedom and those of reaction is certain. The grave plight of the people compels them to resist to the death the stinking policies of the gangsters that rule the country....

We have won important victories. The general political level of the people has been considerably raised and they are now more conscious of their strength. Action has become the language of the day. The ties between the working people and the [African National] Congress have been greatly strengthened.... Here in South Africa, as in many parts of the world, a revolution is maturing; it is the profound desire, the determination and the urge of the overwhelming majority of the country to destroy forever the shackles of oppression that condemn them to servitude and slavery. To overthrow oppression has been sanctioned by humanity and is the highest aspiration of every free man.

On Trial

In response to the mob actions in the east, the government cracked down with more repressive laws and actions, making civil disobedience, including passive resistance, a crime. The Public Safety Act allowed the government to declare martial law and to detain people without trial, and the Criminal Laws Amendment Act authorized corporeal punishment for those who defied the government.

In addition, the government struck out at the organizers of the campaign, including Mandela. On July 30, 1952, at the height of the protest, Mandela was arrested along with twenty-one others, including the presidents and secretaries-general of the major organizations participating in the campaign. With its leaders now in jail, the Defiance Campaign came to a premature end.

Mandela and the others were tried in September 1952 in Johannesburg. Massive crowds of demonstrators marched through the streets of the city during their trial. However heartening this was, Mandela was saddened when ANC president J.S. Moroka broke from the other defendants and offered a plea of mitigation to the court, renouncing the actions of the Defiance Campaign. Further, Moroka betrayed several of the defendants by pointing out Communists—and therefore criminals under the law—amongst his fellow ANC members. Mandela decried the act and knew that whatever the fate of the prisoners, it marked the end of Moroka's presidency.

On December 2, 1952, all of the Defiance Campaign members were found guilty of "statutory communism," meaning those who opposed the government. They were all sentenced to nine months' imprisonment at hard labor, but the sentence was suspended for two years.

Mandela emerged from the trial having led the ANC through its first national campaign against the government. He had earned his status as a freedom fighter and returned to work for the struggle knowing that greater challenges were to come.

Chapter Four

FREEDOM FIGHTER

During the 1950s Mandela's commitment to the struggle against the racist policies of the apartheid government was tested as the government made dissension increasingly dangerous. During this decade, Mandela's actions as a freedom fighter made him a renowned public figure and hero. However, in the eyes of the government and its supporters he was at first a threat and finally a notorious criminal. As a result, the government repeatedly banned Mandela during the 1950s, restricting his movements and freedom to associate with others. Eventually they brought him up on criminal charges for which he twice stood trial.

Mandela and Tambo, Attorneys at Law

The government first banned Mandela in 1952, along with fifty-two other ANC leaders from around the country, for his participation in the 1950 Defiance Campaign. Banning meant that one could not attend any meetings or gatherings—even social or family events—for a period of time and one's movements were restricted to his or her city of residence. Mandela's bans were for six months, coinciding with the ANC's 1952 annual conference during which the now unpopular Dr. Moroka was replaced by Chief Albert Lithuli as ANC president and Mandela was appointed deputy president of the National ANC.

While his bans curtailed his ability to actively fulfill his duties with the ANC, Mandela did his best to pursue his professional career. After failing several attempts, he passed his law exams in 1952 and opened a practice with Oliver Tambo in downtown Johannesburg. The two attorneys specialized in representing Africans and were immediately besieged with clients to the point that every morning Mandela and Tambo had to climb over people waiting outside their offices to see them.

Mandela, in and out of court, was frequently treated with disrespect by whites. Nonetheless, he was a good attorney and championed cases of injustice, police brutality, and other violations brought on Africans by the white government. He was outspoken and flamboyant, given to dramatic speeches and gestures in court.

A Hot-Tempered Advocate

Mandela was equally if not more impassioned and dramatic in his actions and speeches in the ANC's political struggle. Although the ANC advocated nonviolent resistance, Mandela felt that the time for nonviolence was coming to an end and often said so in public. During one speech in 1953, Mandela openly condemned the government for its brutality and said that the time for passive resistance had ended.

Mandela's words made him a dangerous man in the eyes of the government. He was banned for a second time in September 1953, this time for a two-year period. It was a great blow to Mandela because it removed him from the ANC struggle for an extensive period. He devoted his energies to his law practice and bided his time until his bans expired.

The Freedom Charter and the Congress of the People

In reaction to the increasingly brutal and aggressive actions by the government, in 1955 ANC president Chief Lithuli convened a national convention called the Congress of the People. Its purpose was to draw up a document—called the Freedom Charter—laying out principles for a new nonracial government in South Africa. The congress included three thousand delegates representing more than two hundred organizations, black, white, Indian, and colored.

In 1955 ANC president Chief Lithuli convened a national convention called the Congress of the People.

Based on suggestions solicited from around the country, Mandela and others on the National Executive Committee drafted the Freedom Charter and presented it to the Congress of the People in June 1955. The Freedom Charter called for government by the people, equal rights for all, including those to vote, freely purchase and own land, and participate in the country's natural wealth. When presenting it, Mandela said, "The Charter is more than a mere list of demands for democratic reforms; it is a revolutionary document precisely because the changes it envisages cannot be won without breaking up the economic and political set-up of present South Africa."[28]

Treason

Three months after the Congress of the People, police conducted the largest raid in the history of South Africa. At dawn, police raided hundreds of homes looking for evidence of what they considered treason, sedition, or violations of the law. Mandela's home was among the ones searched. Soon after the raid, Mandela was banned for a third time, for a period of five years, and in the following months forty-eight members—nearly the entire ANC leadership—were also banned.

Then, on December 5, 1956, police woke Mandela at his home at dawn and arrested him under the charge of high treason against the South African government for his participation in the Defiance Campaign and the Congress of the People. Almost the entire executive leadership of the ANC was arrested, as were the leaders of numerous other groups. Together, there were 156 men arrested—105 African, 21 Indian, 23 white, and 7 colored.

The Treason Trial

The defendants were accused of high treason and conspiracy to use violence to overthrow the government and replace it with a Communist state. The charges included acts committed between October 1, 1952, and December 13, 1956, including the Defiance Campaign, and various other protests against the apartheid government, as well as the participation in the Congress of the People. If convicted, the defendants faced long prison terms or even the death penalty.

The government's case was founded primarily on the language of the Freedom Charter, which it said was treasonous; however, the defense responded to the government's charges by asserting that although the ideas and beliefs set forth in the charter were repugnant to the present government, they were shared by the overwhelming majority of the citizens of South Africa and the majority of humanity. As Mandela later wrote, the defendants hoped that the trial would not only prove their innocence of the charges of treason but also show that the trial was a political trial in which the government

Against American Imperialism

During the 1950s Mandela regularly wrote articles for the Johannesburg periodical
Liberation. *In the following excerpt from an article titled "A New Menace in Africa," published*
in the March 1958 edition and reprinted on the African National Congress Website
(www.anc.org.za), Mandela discusses the threat he saw posed by U.S. economic interests in
Africa.

American interest in Africa has in recent years grown rapidly. This continent is rich
in raw minerals. It produces almost all the world's diamonds, 78 percent of its palm oil,
68 percent of its cocoa, half of its gold, and 22 percent of its copper. It is rich in man-
ganese, chrome, in uranium, radium, in citrus fruits, coffee, sugar, cotton, and rubber. It is
regarded by the U.S.A. as one of the most important fields of investment....

[Since 1954] the American government has mounted a terrific diplomatic and
economic offensive in almost every part of Africa.... Today, American imperialism is a
serious danger to the independent states in Africa, and its people must unite before it
is too late and fight it out to the bitter end.

American imperialism is all the more dangerous because, having witnessed the
resurgence of the people of Asia and Africa against imperialism and having seen the
decline and fall of once powerful empires, it comes to Africa elaborately disguised.... It
maintains that the huge sums of dollars invested in Africa are not for the exploitation
of the people of Africa but for the purpose of developing their countries and in order
to raise their living standards.... The big and powerful American trade monopolies that
are springing up in various parts of the continent and which are destroying the small
trader, the low wages paid the ordinary man, the resulting poverty and misery, his illiteracy and the squalid tenements in which he dwells are the simplest and most elo-
quent exposition of the falsity of the argument that American investments in Africa
will raise the living standards of the people of this continent.

The American brand of imperialism is imperialism all the same in spite of the mod-
ern clothing in which it is dressed and in spite of the sweet language spoken by its
advocates and agents.... American capital has been sunk into Africa not for the purpose of raising the material standards of its people but in order to exploit them as well
as the natural wealth of their continent. This is imperialism in the true sense of the
word.

was persecuting the prisoners for actions that were morally justified.

The initial drama of the opening arguments was thrilling to the attorney in Mandela; however, the excitement wore off as the hearing dragged on for thirteen months. During the trial the prosecution submitted evidence and presented witnesses to prove that there was sufficient evidence for the case to be heard by the Transvaal Supreme Court, where the defendants would

All 156 of these people, including Mandela, were arrested for treason against the South African government in December 1956. Their trials dragged on for years.

TREASON TRIAL

The ACCUSED

DECEMBER 1956

face the strictest penalties. When the prosecution's presentation of evidence concluded, the judge decided that there was sufficient reason for the case to be heard by the high court. However, by this point, the prosecution had dismissed charges against sixty-one of the defendants, most of whom were minor figures in the ANC and other organizations. Chief Lithuli and Oliver Tambo, two of the highest-ranking ANC members, were also dismissed. Mandela was bewildered by their release but was nonetheless pleased.

Meeting Winnie

A trial date would not be set for months, so the defendants were released to await their next hearing. Mandela returned to his law practice with Oliver Tambo and worked hard to catch up on all the work he had been unable to do during the trial. However, not all of his time away from court was consumed by business and politics.

Soon after his third banning in 1955, Mandela's wife, Evelyn, had separated from him and took their three children with her. Their marriage, which had been deteriorating for many months, ended when Evelyn delivered an ultimatum that Mandela choose her or the ANC. He chose the ANC and the struggle. After his family left, he saw his kids whenever he could, but his banning orders made it difficult.

Then, in December 1955, during an earlier recess in the preliminary examination, Mandela met a young social worker named Nomzamo Winifred Madikizela, known as Winnie, when she came to his office seeking legal counsel for her brother. Mandela was struck by her beauty. "I was thinking more of how I could ask her out than how our firm would handle our case," he later wrote. "I cannot say for certain if there is such a thing as love at first sight, but I do know that the moment I first glimpsed Winnie Nomzamo, I knew that I wanted to have her as my wife."[29] And, on their first date, he told her so.

The couple dated for several months during the break from the trial. Mandela made it clear to Madikizela that he was committed to the struggle against apartheid and if they wed, their marriage would suffer lean times and frequent separation. Additionally, for as long as the trial continued, they would have to rely on her small salary as a social worker since he would have to be in court every day of his trial, unable to earn a living for them.

Despite the uncertain conditions of their future, Madikizela agreed to marry him. On June 14, 1958, shortly after his divorce from Evelyn was finalized, the couple married. After the wedding, the Mandelas moved into his house in Orlando West, which was empty since Evelyn had taken the children to live in the Transkei. By October, Winnie Mandela was pregnant.

The Trial Continues

The celebratory atmosphere of their wedding was soon eclipsed by Mandela's return to court. Their daily routine was dominated by the trial, which commenced in August 1958 and lasted more than three years. The trial was so lengthy that during it Winnie Mandela became pregnant and gave birth to both of the couple's two children, both girls. Zenani (nicknamed Zeni) was born in February 1959 and Zindziswa in winter 1960. Mandela was unable to contribute much time to their upbringing because, when not in court, he was either in his office trying to earn income for his family or at political meetings. As Mandela had warned his wife, his domestic life had to come last.

The inconvenience worsened when the government announced that the trial would be moved to Pretoria, a township thirty-six miles from Johannesburg. Since all of the defendants and their attorneys lived in Johannesburg, it meant a five-hour round-trip commute each day for them, making it even more difficult for the defendants to earn a living during the long trial.

Over the course of the next year, the preliminary arraignment in Pretoria moved slowly. During that time, charges against all but thirty of the remaining defendants were dropped, and finally, on August 3, 1959, two years and eight months after their arrests, the actual trial commenced. Again, the state presented its case and

its witnesses over the course of months, which took until March 10, 1960.

Four days later the defense opened its case, bringing its defense witnesses to the stand, most of them ANC members. Then, on March 21, during testimony by Chief Lithuli, the trial was interrupted by dire news.

Sharpeville

In early March an African antiapartheid group called the Pan Africanist Congress (PAC) had launched a protest against pass laws. These laws required every African over sixteen years of age to carry documents proving their identity, which allowed them to move about the country. Mandela and the ANC had held a similar campaign earlier and had invited the PAC to join, but the rival organization was hostile toward the ANC because the congress admitted non-African members. The PAC refused the alliance.

Large demonstrations were held and met by armed police, the most violent clash occurring in the township of Sharpeville, thirty-five miles south of Johannesburg. Seventy-five police officers confronted the unarmed crowd of several thousand and opened fire, shooting more than seven hundred rounds into the crowd, killing sixty-nine Africans, most of whom were shot in the back as they were fleeing. The police also wounded more than four hundred others, many of them women and children.

"No Bed of Roses"

In his book, Nelson Mandela, *biographer Martin Meredith describes Nelson and Winnie Mandela's wedding, a celebration mixed with foreboding because it took place while Mandela was on trial for high treason and facing a possible death sentence.*

The wedding took place in Bizana on 14 June 1958, a year after they had first met. Mandela had to obtain special permission to leave Johannesburg for six days. The ceremony was held at a local church, with Winnie wearing a wedding gown of white satin.... At a reception at the Bizana Town Hall [Winnie's father] spoke of his love for his daughter and of Mandela's dangerous career as a politician. He expressed deep foreboding for the future: "This marriage will be no bed of roses; it is threatened from all sides and only the deepest love will preserve it." He advised his daughter, "Be like your husband, become like his people and as one with them. If they be witches, become one with them."

After all the feasts and dancing at Bizana, there was no time for Mandela and Winnie to travel on to his ancestral home in Thembuland to continue the celebrations, as custom required. So Winnie wrapped up a piece of wedding cake and took it back to [their house at] no. 8115, Orlando West, intending that she and her husband would share it with his family on a later visit when his restrictions were lifted. It was a journey they never made.

Mandela and his second wife Winnie were married in 1958.

The bodies of more than fifty of the Sharpeville protesters lie dead, murdered by South African police in 1960.

The incident became known as the Sharpeville Massacre and was front-page news all over the world the next day. Protests and admonishments came from all over the world, including from the United States. The uproar even affected the South African economy, causing the stock exchange to plummet.

Anticipating a crackdown by the government on the ANC, the leadership sent ANC secretary-general Oliver Tambo out of the country to avoid his imprisonment. Tambo crossed the border illegally and, with the help of the Indian government, was sent to Britain.

Mandela met with several members from the ANC and other parties to discuss how they should respond to the incident. They spent the entire night talking and finally decided to hold a national day of mourning and protest in concert with a stay-at-home strike on March 28. The event was a success, with several hundred thousand people participating. Additionally, Mandela and Chief

Lithuli publicly burned their pass cards and thousands of others followed suit.

State of Emergency

Rioting accompanied the strike in many areas, and to combat the upheaval, on March 30 the government declared a national state of emergency. Martial law ruled, allowing the government to suspend most of the civil protections of South African citizens, particularly the nonwhites. At 1:30 A.M. police arrived at Mandela's home and arrested him without warrant. Meanwhile, twenty-two thousand other people across the country were also similarly arrested.

Mandela was taken to a police station in what remained of Sophiatown, where he was put in a crowded, stench-ridden cell with many of his ANC colleagues. They were not fed for twelve hours and were given thin, filthy bedding material to use to sleep on the floor. Mandela and his colleagues were detained for thirty-six hours before being called back to Pretoria to attend the treason trial. They were kept in a prison in Pretoria for the duration of the state of emergency, where the conditions were not much better. The ANC's plight worsened even more dramatically on April 1. Under the Unlawful Organization Act, the ANC and the PAC were banned, meaning they were effectively illegal and all of the members of the groups instantly became criminals.

The National Action Council

The treason trial resumed on April 25, 1960, and lasted until March 29, 1961, well beyond the state of emergency, which ended in August 1960. Days prior to the end of the trial, Mandela's third ban expired and he was able to attend meetings outside Johannesburg, including an emergency conference of fourteen hundred delegates at the All-in Conference. This meeting was called to oppose the South African government's intentions to declare itself a whites-only republic on May 31.

At the All-in Conference, the National Action Council (NAC) was formed with Mandela as its leader. The purpose of the NAC was to campaign for a national convention to create a nonracial constitution for South Africa based on the principles of the Freedom Charter. In his first act as leader, Mandela sent a demand to the government that a convention be held before May 31. "If the government ignores us," he said, "we will stage countrywide demonstrations on the eve of the Republic."[30]

We, the People

Drafted by Nelson Mandela and others in the ANC and based on suggestions from people across the country, the Freedom Charter was intended to serve as the basis for a new non-racist South African government. The document, including this preamble, reprinted here from the ANC website, was adopted by the Congress of the People on June 26, 1955.

We, the People of South Africa, declare for all our country and the world to know:

that South Africa belongs to all who live in it, black and white, and that no government can justly claim authority unless it is based on the will of all the people; that our people have been robbed of their birthright to land, liberty and peace by a form of government founded on injustice and inequality; that our country will never be prosperous or free until all our people live in brotherhood, enjoying equal rights and opportunities;

that only a democratic state, based on the will of all the people, can secure to all their birthright without distinction of colour, race, sex or belief; And therefore, we, the people of South Africa, black and white together equals, countrymen and brothers adopt this Freedom Charter; And we pledge ourselves to strive together, sparing neither strength nor courage, until the democratic changes here set out have been won.

Fugitive

After it was outlawed, the ANC survived clandestinely through secret communications and meetings. At one of these meetings, the leadership determined that if Mandela was not convicted during the treason trial, he should go underground and travel around the country to make speeches and organize support for the national convention. Mandela accepted his assignment, but not without worry and regret as it meant leaving Winnie and his family. "This would be a hazardous life," he said, "and I would be apart from my family, but when a man is denied the right to live the life he believes in, he has no choice but to become an outlaw."[31]

On March 29, 1961, Mandela and the remaining twenty-six defendants awaited the verdict of the treason trial, five years after their arrests. In its decision, the court surprised many by dismissing the charges against all of the defendants, with the magistrates ruling:

> On the evidence before this court, it is impossible for this court to come to the conclusion that the ANC had acquired or adopted a policy to overthrow the State by violence, i.e. in the sense that the masses had been prepared or conditioned to commit direct acts of violence against the State.[32]

The verdict was cause for celebration all over the country. Demonstrators flocked to the court. However, Mandela had mixed feelings. He emerged from the trial knowing that times were only going to get worse in South Africa and that he would continue to fight at any cost. He braced himself for a new existence as a revolutionary and a fugitive.

Chapter Five

REVOLUTIONARY

In the early 1960s, working underground as a revolutionary and a fugitive, Mandela successfully shifted the ANC's tactics toward militant action. This radical departure from nonviolence transformed the ANC and Mandela and led to him becoming the most-wanted man in South Africa. The manhunt for Mandela continued until his capture in 1962, following which he endured yet another trial for his life.

The Black Pimpernel

Not wanting to give the police a chance to arrest him or ban him again, immediately after his acquittal at the treason trial Mandela went into hiding at the first of many safe houses he would inhabit over the next months. Mandela adjusted well to living as a fugitive. To

him, it did not seem much different than the life a black man had to live daily in South Africa: "Under apartheid, a black man lived in a shadowy life between legality and illegality, between openness and concealment. To be a black man in South Africa meant not to trust anything, which was not unlike living underground for one's entire life."[33]

During his time underground, Mandela stayed in vacant apartments and in the houses of people sympathetic to the ANC's cause, going outside only at night and even then disguising himself as a servant or a laborer. He traveled around in secret, making unannounced speeches at gatherings and repeatedly foiling police plans to catch him. His elusive exploits caught the imagination of the press, which dubbed him "the Black Pimpernel," after the fictional revolutionary the Scarlet Pimpernel, who evaded capture during the French Revolution.

National Strike

While Mandela lived underground, he saw his family infrequently and at great risk, so he spent most of his time alone. However, he enjoyed the isolation, which gave him time to plot and think about the struggle. He also continued to appear around the country to gain support for an ANC-led national strike planned for May 29–31, 1961.

To intimidate people from participating in the strike, the government displayed its military might for weeks leading up to the date, making it clear that violent retaliation could be expected for civil disobedience. Tanks drove through the streets, helicopters harassed black townships, and police officers and soldiers marched in unprecedented numbers through towns and cities.

When the strike came, hundreds of thousands of Africans risked jobs and homes by participating on the first day. In the Cape, they were joined by Indians and colored workers as well. In a radio address, Mandela praised the participants for "defying unprecedented intimidation by the state, trailed and hounded . . . denied the right to hold meetings, operating in areas heavily patrolled by police and teaming with spies and informants."[34]

However, privately Mandela was disappointed in the turnout for the strike and called it off on its second day. The government was preparing for another massacre, and the people, he knew, could be provoked into violence. In his radio address, Mandela added soberly, "If the government reaction is to crush by naked force our non-violent struggle, we will have to reconsider our tactics. In my mind we are closing a chapter on this question of a non-violent policy."[35]

After being acquitted of treason in 1961, Mandela went into hiding and lived as a fugitive.

The M-Plan

In December 1952, believing that the government would soon outlaw the ANC, Mandela devised a new model of organization and communication for the group that he hoped would allow it to successfully operate clandestinely. In his autobiography Long Walk to Freedom, *Mandela describes the model, which became known as the Mandela Plan, or the M-Plan.*

The idea was to set up organizational machinery that would allow the ANC to make decisions at the highest level, which could then be swiftly transmitted to the organization as a whole without calling a meeting. In other words, it would allow an illegal organization to function and enable leaders who were banned to continue to lead. . . . I . . . came up with a system that was broad enough to adapt itself to local conditions and not fetter individual initiative, but detailed enough to facilitate order. The smallest unit was the cell, which in urban townships consisted of roughly ten houses on a street. A cell steward would be in charge of each of these units. . . . A group of streets formed a zone directed by a chief steward, who was in turn responsible to the secretariat of the local branch of the ANC. The secretariat was a subcommittee of the branch executive, which reported to the provincial secretary. My notion was that every cell and street steward should know every person and family in his area, so that he would be trusted by the people and would know whom to trust. The cell steward arranged meetings, organized political classes, and collected dues. . . . The plan was accepted . . . but it was instituted with only modest success and its adoption was never widespread. . . . The plan faced many problems: it was not always adequately explained to the membership; there were no paid organizers to help implement or administer it; and there was often dissension within the branches. . . . To some, the government's crackdown did not seem imminent, so they did not take the precautions necessary. . . . When the government's iron fist did descend, they were not prepared.

Spear of the Nation

Following the strike, Mandela proposed a plan to develop a military wing to the ANC to force the government into negotiations. He argued that nonviolence was not working. Many in the ANC opposed the plan, including Chief Lithuli, who was an adamant pacifist; however, even Lithuli recognized the truth of Mandela's argument. After much debate, the ANC agreed that Mandela should proceed with his plans. Yet to prevent the ANC from being linked with violence, the military wing would be organized and operated outside the ANC itself, with Mandela as its commander. Mandela later wrote:

> This was a fateful step. For fifty years, the ANC had treated nonviolence as a core principle, beyond question or debate. Henceforth, the ANC would be a different kind of organization. We were embarking on a new and more dangerous path, a path of organized violence, the results of which we did not and could not know.[36]

That autumn, Mandela moved to Rivonia, a rural and sparsely populated suburb of Johannesburg, and set up a base for the new wing at a farm called Liliesleaf. The rural surroundings eventually made it possible for him to go outside during the day. As Mandela recalls, "I naturally found Rivonia an ideal place for the man who lived the life of an outlaw."[37] There, along with other ANC colleagues who came to visit, Mandela laid the plans for the new organization, called Umkhonto we Sizwe, meaning "Spear of the Nation," and also known as MK.

First Attacks

Mandela had to decide on what kind of violence the MK would commit. There were four types of violent activities: sabotage, guerrilla warfare, terror-

ism, and open revolution. He eventually decided on sabotage. He later wrote:

> Our strategy was to make selective forays against military installations, power plants, telephone lines, and transportation links; targets that would not only hamper the military effectiveness of the state, but frighten National Party supporters, scare away foreign capital, and weaken the economy. This we hoped would bring the government to the bargaining table.[38]

Mandela was adamant that people should never be hurt by the sabotage. His goal was the eventual cohabitation of whites and nonwhites, and he felt that if their organization killed anyone, particularly whites, such future cohabitation would be impossible. However, he resolved that if sabotage did not accomplish their aims, they would change to more extreme tactics. "We were prepared to move on to the next stage: guerilla warfare and terrorism."[39]

The MK made its first attack on December 16, 1961. The organization exploded several bombs at electric power stations and vacant government offices in Johannesburg, Port Elizabeth, and Durban. The government and many white South Africans were shocked by the attacks.

Gathering Support

The following month Mandela illegally left South Africa to tour the rest of Africa and Europe to gather financial support and enlist promises of military training for MK soldiers. He was smuggled over the border out of South Africa by car and was then flown into central Africa. Having never been outside South Africa before, Mandela was surprised and pleased at how he was treated by people of other races. He says, "For the first time in my life I was a free man; free from white oppression, from the idiocy of apartheid and racial arrogance, from police molestation, from humiliation and indignity. Wherever I went I was treated like a human being."[40]

His support mission was an educational experience for him, but it was only partly successful in its goals. Many African nations, even those that were former colonies themselves, were not eager to support violent uprising. Mandela was given money by several nations but nothing else. However, Algeria and Ethiopia agreed to help with military training.

After a brief visit to Europe, where he met with Oliver Tambo, Mandela returned to Ethiopia and received soldier's training—something he felt he was sorely lacking as a leader. He learned how to use an automatic rifle and a pistol, learned about explosives, and how generally to think like a soldier. He wanted to be able to rise to the occasion of military action when it was necessary.

"If there was to be guerilla warfare," he recounts, "I wanted to be able to stand and fight with my people and to share the hazards of war with them."[41]

Although his training was supposed to last six months, two months into it he received a telegram calling him back to South Africa. It said that the internal armed struggle in South Africa was escalating and the MK needed its commander. As a farewell gesture, the Ethiopian government presented Mandela with an automatic pistol and two hundred rounds of ammunition, which he smuggled back into South Africa along with the money he had collected.

Captured

Mandela sneaked back into South Africa and reported to the Working Committee of the MK at the Liliesleaf farm. He gave his colleagues a general overview of his travels and itemized the money and offers of training he had gathered.

The committee, eager for Chief Lithuli to hear Mandela's report, told Mandela to deliver his news in person in Durban the following day. However, on August 5, 1962, while en route, his car was pulled over by police officers who had been tipped off by an informant of his return. He was arrested and charged with inciting the May 1961 strike and leaving the country without a passport. The government at this point did not charge him for his military actions as part of the MK.

Mandela's wife Winnie, (foreground) and other supporters arrive at Mandela's 1962 trial in Pretoria. Winnie Mandela helped to raise funds for her husband's defense.

Mandela's initial hearing began on October 15, 1962, in Pretoria. Mandela defended himself with friend and Communist Party member Joe Slovo serving as a legal adviser. Meanwhile, colleagues and activists set up a Free Mandela! fund to help raise money for his defense as well as that of other political detainees.

At the beginning of his hearing, Mandela addressed the court and shocked the judges by accusing the South African judicial system of racism and prejudice:

Why is it that in this courtroom I am facing a white magistrate, confronted by a white prosecutor, escorted by white orderlies? Can anybody honestly and seriously suggest that in this type of atmosphere the scales of justice are evenly balanced? Why is it that no African in the history of this country has ever had the honor of being tried by his own kith and kin . . . ? Your Worship, I hate racial discrimination most intensely and in all its manifestations. I have fought it all my life. I fight it now, and will do so until the end of my days.[42]

Despite his protest, the prosecution proceeded with its case against him, presenting a hundred witnesses, including policemen, journalists, superintendents of townships, and others, all of whom gave evidence to show that Mandela had incited the May 1961 national strike. They also provided evidence that he had left the country illegally.

In his own testimony, Mandela perplexed the court by admitting to all of the charges against him. Further, once the prosecution rested its case, Mandela declared that he was not calling any witnesses in his defense and rested his case.

Then, on the final day of the trial, Mandela delivered a lengthy and heartfelt closing speech to the court. In it, he explained to the court how he came to be the man he was, why he had done the things he had done in violation of the law, and why he would do them again if given the chance:

I would say that the whole life of any thinking African in this country drives him continuously to a conflict between his conscience on the one hand and the law on the other. . . . Our consciences dictate that we must protest against [the law], that we must oppose it, and that we must attempt to alter it. . . . I was made, by the law, a criminal, not because of what I had done but what I stood for, because of what I thought, because of my conscience. . . . Whatever sentence Your Worship sees fit to impose upon me . . . rest assured that when my sentence has been completed . . . I will still be moved . . . to take up again, as best I can, the struggle for the removal of those injustices until they are finally abolished once and for all.[43]

In spite of the eloquence of his plea, Mandela was found guilty and was sentenced to five years in prison.

The Rivonia Trial

Mandela was taken to prison in Pretoria. Then, at the end of May 1963, after serving seven months, he was moved to Robben Island, a notorious prison on an island eighteen miles off the western coast near Cape Town. Mandela had heard about Robben Island as a child. It

The MK Agenda

Under Mandela's command, Umkhonto we Sizwe's first sabotage attacks against government property were carried out on December 16, 1961, in cities across South Africa. The explosions were accompanied by the distribution of the new group's manifesto in an effort to gain support for the group and explain its tactics and purpose. The following excerpt from the manifesto was reprinted in The Struggle Is My Life, *a collection of Mandela's speeches and writings.*

It is . . . well known that the main national liberation organisations in this country have consistently followed a policy of non-violence. They have conducted themselves peaceably at all times, regardless of government attacks and persecutions upon them, and despite all government-inspired attempts to provoke them to violence. They have done so because the people prefer peaceable methods of change to achieve their aspirations without the suffering and bitterness of civil war. But the people's patience is not endless.

The time comes in the life of any nation when there remain only two choices: submit or fight. That time has now come to South Africa. We shall not submit and we have no choice but to hit back by all means within our power in defence of our people, our future and our freedoms. . . . We of Umkhonto we Sizwe always sought—as the liberation movement has sought—to achieve liberation without bloodshed and civil clash. We do so still. We hope—even at this late hour—that our first actions will awaken everyone to a realisation of the disastrous situation to which the Nationalist policy is leading. We hope that we will bring the government and its supporters to their senses before it is too late. . . . In these actions, we are working in the best interests of all the people of this country— black, brown and white. . . . We appeal for the support and encouragement of all those South Africans who seek the happiness and the freedom of the people of this country.

An aerial view of Robben Island off the western coast of South Africa, where Nelson Mandela spent twenty-six years as a political prisoner.

was where the British had imprisoned Xhosa warriors since the early nineteenth century. On Robben Island, the guards were armed, unfriendly, and spoke Afrikaans, the language of the Boers. They refused to speak English because of its link to Britain.

Mandela was put in isolation with two other political prisoners. After only a few weeks, though, in late July 1963, Mandela was unexpectedly taken back to Pretoria. There, through the grapevine, he learned that the MK base at the Liliesleaf farm in Rivonia had been dis-

covered and raided that month. Police officers had arrested numerous people, including Walter Sisulu and other ANC colleagues. They had also confiscated hundreds of documents, including incriminating ones related to a guerrilla warfare plan not yet executed. Mandela's involvement as leader of the MK high command had been described in numerous documents.

In October 1963 the trial against Mandela and his MK colleagues, which became known as the Rivonia Trial, began in the Palace of Justice in

Pretoria. The defendants, charged with sabotage and guerrilla warfare, faced possible death sentences.

Damning Evidence

Over the next five months the prosecution presented hundreds of witnesses and documents in its case. From the start of the trial, the evidence against the men was overwhelming. The state had convinced a former MK operative to inform, and, as Mandela recalled, the operative's testimony, particularly against Mandela, was devastating.

Further, a document confiscated from the farm in Rivonia outlined the plans for guerrilla operations employing up to seven thousand MK recruits. The defense argued—truthfully—that the operation laid out in the document had not yet been formally adopted and was still under discussion. Nonetheless, it was a particularly damning piece of evidence.

In their defense, Mandela and his codefendants adamantly refused the contention that they had embarked on guerrilla warfare. Further, they would deny claims of murder and damage to innocent bystanders, as the state had accused. However, since they realized the charges against them were serious and that they were likely to be convicted, Mandela and his codefendants decided that they would admit their guilt to certain charges and use the witness box as a pulpit to speak out against the government. Mandela says, "We would not defend ourselves in a legal sense so much as in a moral sense."[44]

Mandela Testifies

Mandela's testimony was first, and he set the tone for the rest of the defense. His statement was lengthy and filled with emotion. He made it clear that the actions he had taken while in the ANC and the MK had been moral and for the struggle for freedom. Further, he acknowledged his part in the creation of the MK and in the planning and execution of the group's actions up until his imprisonment the previous year. He told the court that the choice to commit violence was not terrorism, that it was the goal of the ANC for all people, black and white, to exist in an equal, nonracial society. He gave a brief history of the ANC and the nonviolent struggles they had performed, from the Defiance Campaign through the strikes and protests of the early 1960s, and attested to how the government continually met these peaceful protests with violence. This violence by the government, he said, led to violence by the MK. "It was only when all else had failed, when all channels of peaceful

Borrowing Ideas from the West and the East

During the Rivonia Trial, in an attempt to convict and discredit Mandela, government prosecutors attempted to brand Mandela as a Communist bent on overthrowing the South African government and replacing it with a Communist regime. In the following passage, excerpted from his statement to the court and reprinted in a book published by the International Defence and Aid Fund for Southern Africa, I Am Prepared to Die, *Mandela argues that neither his ideals nor those of the government he hoped to bring about were Communist; they were based on philosophies of the West as much as the East.*

It is true . . . that I have been influenced by Marxist thought. . . . [I] accept the need for some form of socialism to enable our people to catch up with the advanced countries of this world and to overcome their legacy of extreme poverty. But this does not mean we are Marxists. . . .

Communists regard the parliamentary system of the West as undemocratic and reactionary. But, on the contrary, I am an admirer of such a system.

The Magna Carta, the Petition of Rights, and the Bill of Rights are documents which are held in veneration by democrats throughout the world. . . . I regard the British Parliament as the most democratic institution in the world and the impartiality of its judiciary never fail to arouse my admiration.

The American Congress, that country's doctrine of separation of powers, as well as the independence of its judiciary, arouses similar sentiments in me.

I have been influenced in my thinking by both West and East. . . . I should tie myself to no particular system of society other than of socialism. I must leave myself free to borrow the best from the West and from the East.

protest had been barred to us, that the decision was made to embark on violent forms of political struggle, and to form Umkhonto we Sizwe . . . because the Government had left us with no other choice."[45]

Mandela spoke out against the indignities and hardships caused by the racism and oppression of apartheid. He listed grievances of Africans: inequality, lack of access to the riches of their own land, low pay, poverty, malnutrition and disease, inadequate education, pass laws, segregation, the inability to participate in government, and the lack of access to good jobs.

Finally, Mandela concluded with a pledge of his commitment to the struggle, even if it cost him his life:

During my lifetime I have dedicated myself to this struggle. . . . I have cherished the ideal of a democratic and free society in which all persons live together in harmony and with equal opportunities. It is an ideal which I hope to live for and to achieve. But if needs be, it is an ideal for which I am prepared to die.[46]

Verdict

When the other men had concluded their testimony, the defense rested. Then, on June 11, 1964, the court returned a verdict of guilty for Mandela and seven other defendants, including Walter Sisulu, Govan Mbeki, Raymond Mhlaba, Elias Motsoaledi, Andrew Mlangeni, Ahmed Kathrada, and Denis Goldberg. They were each given life sentences.

Mandela's revolutionary stance against the government had brought him to the darkest period yet. As he returned to Robben Island, he struggled to retain hope that he would not spend the rest of his life behind bars.

Chapter Six

PRISONER OF CONSCIENCE

After his conviction in the Rivonia Trial, Mandela faced the prospect of spending decades—perhaps the rest of his life—behind bars. However, his imprisonment itself helped transform Mandela into an international symbol against apartheid and racial injustice.

Immediate international outcry arose in protest of the sentences handed down in the Rivonia Trial. The delegates on the United Nations Security Council voted 106 to 1 (South Africa) for the unconditional release of the prisoners and all other South African political prisoners. However, political attempts by the United Nations to impose sanctions on South Africa as punishment were vetoed by Britain, France, and the United States, and the South African government upheld the sentences of Mandela and his colleagues.

Returning to Robben Island

Shortly after his forty-sixth birthday, Mandela and his colleagues were sent to Robben Island. As political prisoners, they were housed together, isolated from the rest of the prison population for fear they would incite trouble among the other African prisoners. Being housed together alleviated some of the emotional hardship of prison life; however, the distance from home and the physical conditions at Robben Island were harsh. Mandela later recalled:

[The island's] isolation made it not simply another prison, but a world of its own, far removed from the one we had come from. . . . In Pretoria, we felt connected to our supporters and our families; on the island, we felt cut off, and indeed we were. We had the consolation of being with each other, but that was the only consolation.[47]

Soon after their arrival, a new maximum-security section was built for political prisoners with a thirty-foot wall separating them from the other cell blocks. Like those of other inmates, Mandela's cell was seven feet square and furnished only with a mat and two blankets to insulate him from the damp, cold stone floor on which he slept. A dim forty-watt bulb burned twenty-four hours a day and a small one-foot-square window provided the only light inside where he spent almost all of his time for many weeks.

Daily Prison Life

The prison diet was made up of corn, coffee, and a bland soup occasionally enriched by small pieces of meat or vegetables. Whereas the Indian and colored prisoners received a spoonful of

Mandela lived in this prison cell on Robben Island. Located in an isolated wing, Mandela's cell was designed to prevent contact with the general prison population.

Mandela and other Robben Island inmates were forced to break rocks in the hot sun as part of their punishment. Mandela led a strike to protest this practice.

sugar with their morning porridge, the Africans only received half a teaspoon. Additionally, African men were given short pants instead of trousers like other prisoners as a reminder of their demeaned racial status. Mandela protested against wearing the short pants from the start, but it would be years before he would be successful in changing the prison's demeaning policy.

Mandela's daily prison routine was rigorous and laborious. For the first decade he and his friends spent at Robben Island, he would wake at 5:30 A.M. and be rushed through his morning bathing and marched in silence to

breakfast with the rest of the prisoners. From that point on, he was not allowed to speak to anyone until the lunch break.

After breakfast, prisoners were marched off to work until lunch. Following lunch, they worked until 4:30 P.M. and then marched back to the compound, where they were stripped naked and searched. After that, they collected dinner, which they ate in their cells. At this point Mandela and the other prisoners were free to chat among themselves.

Initially, their work was to sit in the prison courtyard and break up large rocks into gravel with small hammers. It was tedious and hard work, and the guards constantly increased the demands of how much gravel the prisoners were to produce, trying to make them work harder and break their spirits. Just as he had done outside the prison, Mandela tried to improve the conditions of Africans. Led by Mandela, the Rivonia convicts staged a go-slow strike. They purposefully worked at less than half the speed to protest the guards' excessive and unfair demands. Although they were threatened by the guards to work faster, the prisoners continued the strike for the duration of the winter.

Bearing Hardships

The hardships of the first years on the island were difficult for Mandela and the others. However, from the first day he spent at Robben Island, Mandela was determined not to let the circumstance of his imprisonment defeat him. According to Mandela:

> The challenge for every prisoner, particularly every political prisoner, is how to survive prison intact, how to emerge from prison undiminished, how to conserve and even replenish one's beliefs. . . . Prison and the authorities conspire to rob each man of his dignity. In and of itself, that assured that I would survive, for any man or institution that tries to rob me of my dignity will lose because I will

not part with it at any price or under any pressure.[48]

Contact with the outside world was almost nonexistent. Prisoners could write only one letter a month and were allowed one visit every six months. Because of the difficulty of getting to the island, however, in reality, visits were often less frequent. Further, all mail was read and censored by the prison authorities. Several letters Mandela received from his wife were all but completely blacked out.

Winnie came to visit Mandela for the first time only weeks after his arrival on the island. The couple sat in a cramped visiting room separated by glass. Mandela recalls how difficult the visits were: "It was tremendously frustrating not to be able to touch my wife, to speak tenderly to her, to have a private moment together. We had to conduct our relationship at a distance under the eyes of people we despised."[49]

Resisting and Organizing

Prisoners were visited occasionally by Red Cross officials, who attempted to ensure that the prisoners were treated humanely. Mandela was elected spokesperson by his colleagues to present their grievances to the officials, and he complained about the poor conditions under which they lived—their clothing, their food, the lack of visitation, the hard labor, and the behavior of the guards, among other things.

Although most conditions did not change, Mandela was able to win study privileges for the prisoners. Many of the men registered for university or high school courses, and Mandela himself pursued postgraduate studies.

In addition to studying, the men struggled to make life better by developing their own supportive community within the prison. Mandela says:

> We had to build our own social life and we modeled it in terms of the life we had lived and would live outside the prison walls. . . . In that constricted, deprived environment, we placed the highest value on sharing, sharing everything, every resource, material and intellectual, and on the whole we succeeded.[50]

Mandela and the others also continued to live by the political principles of resistance that they followed outside prison. Over the years, they engaged in hunger strikes, food boycotts, work slowdowns, and various other tactics of protest against the harsh conditions of the prison.

They also formed their own prison branch of the ANC, which they called the High Organ. Sisulu, Mbeki, Mhlaba, and Mandela served as senior officers, with Mandela as president of the group. The High Organ met secretly and made decisions regarding life in the prison, including protests and internal actions.

Dark Days

Cut off from the outside world, Mandela received little news about the struggle in South Africa. What news he did receive from new prisoners or visitors was usually bleak. By the late 1960s almost all of the senior ANC members were in prison, most of them at Robben Island. Meanwhile, the South African government grew stronger and increasingly ruthless. The MK continued its mission to battle using sabotage and armed struggle, but soon increasing numbers of MK soldiers arrived at Robben Island bearing heavy sentences.

The late 1960s were difficult for Mandela personally as well. Several tragedies in his family struck in close succession. In 1968 he learned that his mother had died. He requested permission to attend the funeral but was denied. Only months later, his oldest son, Makgatho, twenty-five years old and a father of two small children, was killed in an automobile accident. Again, prison officials rejected Mandela's request to attend the funeral. Distraught, Mandela had to cope with the tragedies without the comfort of his wife. During his first years in prison, Winnie Mandela was able to visit only infrequently due to being banned for political activities. Further, in 1969 she was arrested without warrant under the Suppression of Communism Act. She was interrogated and tortured for

An ANC member reads the newspaper in his cell at Robben Island in the 1960s. Once strictly forbidden, newspapers were eventually distributed to prisoners due to Mandela's efforts.

nearly six months before being charged. When Mandela learned of the arrest through a prison guard, he despaired. He recalls, "There was nothing I found so agonizing in prison as the thought that Winnie was in prison too."[51]

Apartheid in Trouble

However bleak things looked on the outside, changes in the country slowly began to occur. In the early 1970s the South African government's apartheid policy met with unprecedented resistance from antiapartheid groups. More promisingly, this resistance was increasingly joined by the South African business community, which was worried over the economic instability caused by apartheid and the violent uprisings in protest to it. For instance, in June 1976 protesters gathered in the township of Soweto in opposition to the government's recent Bantu Education Act, which required half of all classes in secondary schools to be taught in Afrikaans—the language of the Boers and the Afrikaner Nationalist Party—now known as the National Party.

Over fifteen thousand students, many of them young children, led a peaceful protest through the streets of Soweto, which turned violent when police confronted protesters and opened fire on the crowd. The children fought back with sticks and stones, but the protest ended with hundreds of them wounded and two white men stoned to death.

The Soweto uprising triggered mass riots, violence, and school boycotts throughout the country. In response to the news of Soweto and other uprisings, Mandela wrote a letter that was smuggled out and published by Oliver Tambo. It was a call to action and unified resistance:

The evils, the cruelty and the inhumanity of apartheid have been there from the start. . . . The measure of this truth is the recognition by our

people that under apartheid, our lives, individually and collectively, count for nothing. . . . However, the world is on our side . . . [and] between the anvil of mass action and the hammer of the armed struggle we shall crush apartheid and white minority racist rule.[52]

Free Mandela!

In response to the violence set off by the Soweto massacre, the South African government responded with its usual course of retaliation and oppression. However, in September 1978 Prime Minister John Vorster, who had held office for twelve years, stepped down due to a corruption scandal. He was replaced by Pieter Willem Botha, the former minister of defense.

Botha recognized that his presidency must make some changes, at least symbolic ones, to alleviate the growing international animosity toward the South African Government and its apartheid policies. Botha turned his attention to the man who, although he did not know it, was fast becoming a powerful symbol of the antiapartheid movement: Nelson Mandela.

Although his voice had been silenced by his imprisonment for over a decade, by the late 1970s Mandela was still on the minds of antiapartheid activists all over the world. As biographer Fatima Meer writes, "[He had become] internationally celebrated as

Working the Limestone Quarry

Beginning in January 1965 Mandela and his fellow political prisoners were sent to a lime quarry at the center of Robben Island. There, the men dug out limestone by hand and then cut the stone and loaded it on trucks. The intensity of the heat, the dust from the limestone, and the brutality of the work was punishing. However, as he writes in his book Long Walk to Freedom, *although the work was intended to break their spirit, it had the opposite effect.*

The lime quarry looked like an enormous white crater cut into the rocky hillside. The cliffs and the base of the hillside were blindingly white. At the top of the quarry were grass and palm trees, and at the base was a clearing with a few old metal sheds....

Despite the blistered and bleeding hands, we were invigorated. I much preferred being outside in nature, being able to see grass and trees, to observe birds flitting overhead, to feel the wind blowing in from the sea. It felt good to use all of one's muscles, with the sun at one's back, and there was simple gratification in building up mounds of stone and lime.

Within a few days, we were walking to the quarry, rather than going by truck, and this too was a tonic. During our twenty-minute march to the quarry, we got a better sense of the island, and could see the dense brush and tall trees that covered our home, and smell the eucalyptus blossoms, spot the occasional springbok or kudu grazing in the distance. Although some of the men regarded the march as drudgery, I never did.

Mandela and fellow political prisoners were forced to perform back-breaking work at a Robben Island lime quarry.

Police tear gas forces student protesters at Witwatersrand University to disperse. The students' 1980s Free Mandela! campaign garnered global attention.

the human symbol of freedom and human resistance against tyranny."[53]

Gestures of goodwill and solidarity in Mandela's honor poured in from all over the world. In 1979 India awarded him the Nehru Prize, its highest civic award, and the University of London nominated him for chancellorship. Into the early 1980s, universities awarded Mandela honorary degrees, awards were given to him in his absence, and cities renamed parks and streets after him.

One of the most important actions taken in Mandela's name was the 1980 Free Mandela! campaign launched by students at Witwatersrand University. The campaign demonstrated, gathered funds, and issued petitions in an effort to force the government to unconditionally release Mandela. Over fifty-eight thousand South Africans, black and white, signed a petition for the release of Mandela and other political prisoners, and the campaign received key support from the United States and Europe. Further, that year the United Nations Security Council called for Mandela's release.

The pressure on the government worked. In April 1982 Mandela, Sisulu, and three other Rivonia prisoners were suddenly transferred from Robben Island. Without even adequate time to say good-bye to inmates with whom they had spent over a decade, the five men were taken to Pollsmoor maximum security prison in Takia, a suburb of Cape Town. They did not know why they had been moved or how long they would remain there. However, Mandela suspected that the changes were politically motivated.

Changing Tides

Life at the new prison was a great improvement over the conditions at Robben Island. Although the men were segregated from the general prison population, they had the opportunity to read from a variety of newspapers and magazines, listen to the radio, eat better food, and have more regular visitation. During Mandela's first visit at Pollsmoor with Winnie and his daughter Zeni, for the first time in twenty-two years Mandela was able to kiss his wife.

Other less personal visits to Mandela followed. Near the end of 1984 Mandela was visited by a member of the British Parliament, Lord Bethell. The visit had been allowed by the South African government as a publicity measure to show that Mandela, now the country's most famous prisoner, was in good health and being treated well. Visitors from many

nations came to speak with Mandela, and the publicity increased Mandela's celebrity and the attention to the plight of South African political prisoners.

Standing by His Principles

Hoping to use Mandela's celebrity to the benefit of his government, Botha's administration made offers to release Mandela and his colleagues; however, the offers always came with conditions attached. After several private unsuccessful offers, on January 31, 1985, Botha announced publicly that he would release Mandela if Mandela would renounce violence as a means of protest. Botha concluded at the time, "It is not the South African government which now stands in the way of Mr. Mandela's freedom. It is himself."[54]

Although he greatly desired freedom, Mandela refused to accept his release unless it was unconditional. He rejected Botha's offer in a letter that his daughter Zindziswa read before a crowd of ten thousand people in Soweto. In it, Mandela declared that the government needed to give up violence first:

> Let Botha . . . renounce violence. Let him say that he will dismantle apartheid. Let him unban the people's organization, the ANC. . . . I cannot and will not give any undertaking at a time when I and you, the people are not free. Your freedom and mine cannot be separated.[55]

The government was angered and disappointed by Mandela's response. Conditions in the country were worse than ever, and it had hoped Mandela's release would quell some of the violence. The worst economic depression in fifty years engulfed the country in 1984, casting tens of thousands into unemployment. Inflation rose, the standard of living worsened for Africans, and droughts devastated farms. Finally, economic sanctions were imposed by the United States, Britain, and other countries, cutting South Africa off from its sources of trade. These harsh condi-

tions were accompanied by widespread crime, rioting, and killing. Some of the bloodiest violence was committed by Africans on other Africans suspected of complicity with the apartheid government.

Talking with the Enemy

Despite his refusals to accept conditional release, the South African government continued to attempt negotiations with Mandela, believing that if it could make symbolic progress with him and his ANC colleagues, the violence could be quelled. In December 1988,

Hoping to benefit from Mandela's celebrity status, South African prime minister Pieter Willem Botha offered Mandela a conditional release in 1985.

Winnie's Troubles

During Mandela's decades of imprisonment, his wife Winnie was besieged by continual harassment, arrests, and bannings. She was banned for all but two weeks from 1962 to 1975. In 1969 she was detained and then imprisoned in solitary confinement at Pretoria Center Prison under the Suppression of Communism Act for promoting the aims of the then-illegal ANC. Because of her circumstances, she had to send her daughters away to school in Swaziland—out of the country—because South African school officials repeatedly found reasons to expel them.

When her bans expired in 1975 and were not renewed for the first time in thirteen years, Winnie Mandela helped organize the Black Women's Federation and in 1976 the Black Parents' Association to assist people with medical and legal problems caused by the Soweto riots. However, in August 1976 the police arrested her along with thousands of other activists, holding her until December. Then, in May 1977, she was banned and also banished from her home in the Orlando township. She was restricted to a township on the outskirts of Brandfort in the Orange Free State, a white Afrikaner racist stronghold. She remained confined to the area under twenty-four-hour surveillance by police who enforced the restrictions of her bans, including not allowing her to meet with more than one person at a time.

She returned to Orlando against her banning orders in 1985, when someone fire-bombed her Brandfort house. The government eventually lifted her restrictions.

after a brief hospitalization for a case of tuberculosis brought on by the dampness of his prison cell, the government transferred Mandela from Pollsmoor to Victor Verster, a prison outside of Cape Town, where he was given a private house as a residence. Government officials hoped the privacy and isolation would facilitate negotiations.

Although Mandela had some misgivings about secretly negotiating with the government, he decided to keep the talks from his colleagues in the ANC because he felt he was putting the organization's credibility at risk by agreeing to talk with the enemy. He says:

> There are times when a leader must move out ahead of the flock, go off in a new direction, confident that he is leading his people the right way. Finally, my isolation furnished my organization with an excuse in case matters went awry: the old man was alone and completely cut off.[56]

De Klerk

After numerous meetings with lesser government officials, Mandela was told that he would get the chance to speak with Prime Minister Botha. However, on July 5, 1989, when Mandela was driven in secret to Botha's presidential palace, Botha had drawn back from the idea of negotiating with Africans and only engaged in small talk, never bringing up politics. Then, surprisingly, a month later Botha appeared on television and publicly resigned from office after having been forced out by his own cabinet members.

Despite the setback, Mandela was initially pleased with Botha's successor, F.W. de Klerk. In his inaugural ad-dress, de Klerk said his government was committed to peace and would negotiate with any other group committed to the same. Soon afterward, he allowed a peaceable protest march in Cape Town to be carried out without incident. This, to Mandela, was a sign that de Klerk was a very different leader from those in the past.

Through correspondence, Mandela urged de Klerk's new government to display its good intentions by releasing

South African prime minister F.W. de Klerk negotiated with the imprisoned Mandela. De Klerk ordered Mandela's unconditional release in February 1990.

his fellow prisoners at Pollsmoor and Robben Island without condition. In response, on October 10, 1989, de Klerk did just that. All of the prisoners were released. Mandela was pleased and appreciative but continued to press the prime minister toward further action.

Freedom

On December 13, 1989, Mandela met with de Klerk in secret and the two men immediately discussed politics. Mandela found the new prime minister reasonable and serious but not willing to give in to all of Mandela's demands. After their meeting, it was clear to Mandela that de Klerk was not about to give up white minority power entirely.

In return, Mandela indicated that even if he were freed, he would go right back to work for the ANC, which was still an illegal organization. He insisted that de Klerk restore the ANC and other opposition groups to legal status. Neither Mandela nor de Klerk committed to any action, and the two men left the meeting with respect for each other but with uncertain ideas about what would happen next.

What did happen astounded Mandela and most of the country. On February 2, 1990, during his opening address to the South African Parliament, de Klerk announced numerous sweeping reforms, including lifting the ban on the ANC, the PAC, the Communist Party, and thirty-one other organizations. He also freed all nonviolent political prisoners, suspended the use of capital punishment, and lifted several restrictions imposed by the 1986 state of emergency. Mandela was awed. He said later, "It was a breathtaking moment, for in one sweeping action, he had virtually normalized the situation in South Africa. Our world had changed overnight."[57]

Within a week, Mandela's personal world also changed drastically. On February 10 Mandela again met with de Klerk, and the prime minister announced that on the following day Mandela would be freed from prison unconditionally. The next day, February 11, 1990, Mandela walked out of Victor Verster Prison a free man for the first time in twenty-seven years.

Prison had changed Mandela's life in dramatic ways, but he still was a freedom fighter. He knew that although he was out of prison, the struggle against apartheid was not over.

Chapter Seven

STATESMAN

After his release from prison, Mandela immediately returned to work for the ANC as deputy president. In the decade that followed, he continued his efforts to bring about meaningful change in his country's government. His goal was the same as it had been when he entered prison: to see South Africa become a nonracial democracy where all people would be equal under the law. In the first speech after his release, he said:

> Today the majority of South Africans, black and white, recognize that apartheid has no future. It has to be ended by our own decisive mass action in order to build peace and security. . . . Our march of freedom is irreversible. We must not allow fear to stand in our way.[58]

In the more than four years of negotiations, setbacks, protests, and violence that followed this speech, Mandela worked tirelessly to end apartheid. Then, in April 1994, his labors and sacrifices were rewarded when he was elected president of South Africa in the country's first democratic elections.

No Time to Rest

Although Mandela wanted to spend some time in the country visiting his home and his mother's grave, the ANC was eager to use the international attention of his release to its advantage. Mandela's calendar was filled for weeks in advance with speeches and meetings designed to continue to pressure Prime Minister de Klerk into negotiations with the ANC and other groups to plan a new democratic government.

In May 1990 early negotiations between the government and the ANC began, with both parties outlining their agendas and concerns, including actions they promised to take to make wider and more substantive talks possible. Meanwhile, both de Klerk and Mandela toured Western countries. While de Klerk lobbied for the end to sanctions, Mandela pressed countries to retain them until apartheid had ended.

Mandela visited the United States, where he spoke to President George H.W. Bush and a joint session of both houses of Congress. Next he went to Britain to speak to Parliament and Prime Minister Margaret Thatcher. In both countries he made it clear that although de Klerk's administration was making more progress than any before it in fifty years, the pillars of apartheid still stood—many political prisoners still remained in jail, the apartheid laws still existed, and the fundamental rights of citizenship had not been given to the mass of the people. According to Mandela, "We still have a struggle on our hands. Our common and noble efforts to abolish the system of white minority domination must continue. . . . Sanctions should remain in place. The purpose for which they were imposed has not yet been achieved."[59]

Obstacles to Negotiations

Early progress in negotiations was impeded by numerous obstacles. The largest of these was the widespread violence that had engulfed the country in the late 1980s and still raged on, even under the remaining state of emergency restrictions. With the country in a state of chaos and violence, the government felt it could not openly negotiate with the ANC without alienating the whites in the country.

Mandela's ANC and de Klerk's government worked together to end apartheid.

Much of the violence in South Africa was incited by a rival party to the ANC called the Inkatha Freedom Party (IFP). Created by a former ANC Youth League member and the chief minister of the Kwa Zulu homeland, Mangosuthu Gatssha Buthelezi, the IFP was made up primarily of rural, uneducated Zulus who, under Buthelezi opposed the direction of the ANC. Although Buthelezi had been one of the men calling for Mandela's release from prison and had himself refused negotiations with the government before Mandela was released, Buthelezi's followers had engaged in brutal attacks on ANC members during Mandela's last years in prison. Between 1986 and 1990, more than four thousand people had been killed in the violence.

The government had made matters worse by making it legal for Zulus to carry so-called traditional weapons

Zulu leader Mangosuthu Gatssha Buthelezi was the head of the Inkatha Freedom Party that incited Zulus to resist the South African government through violent means.

such as spears, machetes, and knives in public, which they used in attacks against ANC members. While the government argued that it had legalized the weapons for cultural reasons, Mandela and others in the ANC suspected it had been because the government still viewed the ANC as an enemy and believed that any violence directed toward the group would inevitably help the government.

Soon after Mandela returned from the United States and Britain in July 1990, the IFP held a rally in the township of Sebekong, just outside Johannesburg. After the rally the Zulus rampaged, killing thirty-two people, mostly ANC members. Mandela was angered because the government had done nothing to prevent the violence, and it did not attempt to arrest the perpetrators afterward. Mandela wrote to de Klerk, chastising him: "In any other country where 32 people had been slaughtered in this way, the head of state would come out condemning the matter and giving sympathies to the next of kin."[60]

Government Conspiracy

Mandela and others in the ANC suspected that not only was the government not doing anything to prevent the violence but also that it may have been assisting the IFP in its attacks. Police were accused of refusing to disarm Inkatha attackers and of standing by while the attacks took place. Then,

in September 1990, a group of six IFP members attacked a commuter train, randomly shooting passengers and then following survivors out onto the platform and continuing the assault there. Twenty-six people died and more than a hundred were injured. The attack made the ANC suspicious of the government because it was similar to the kind of terrorist activity carried out for years in Mozambique by rebels trained and supported by South African military intelligence.

In spite of his suspicions, Mandela continued to deal with de Klerk, feeling that he was still the greatest hope for eventually moving the country toward a democratic and nonracial government. At times, it seemed as if his trust was well placed. In February 1991 de Klerk promised to introduce legislation to repeal several of the strongest of the apartheid laws. De Klerk kept his promise and was rewarded by U.S. president Bush, who removed sanctions against South Africa.

However, the IFP violence persisted, and Mandela came to believe that there was a right-wing conspiracy within the government bent on destroying the negotiations with the ANC. He even believed that de Klerk personally was involved in encouraging the violence of ANC opponents.

Mandela continued negotiations with de Klerk out of necessity; however, as biographer Martin Meredith writes, it was never with the same trust: "Mandela never regained his trust of de Klerk. Their relationship henceforth was marked more by abrasive encounters than by signs of cooperation. Mandela now joined others on the national executive committee in advocating a tougher line."[61]

Marital Troubles

Mandela's suspicions that there was a conspiracy in the government against the ANC were compounded in 1991 when Winnie Mandela was charged with being an accessory to murder. During Mandela's imprisonment, Winnie Mandela had organized a group of young men to serve as her bodyguards. Some of them were implicated in the murder of an African boy believed to be a government conspirator. The charges against Winnie Mandela alleged that she too had played a part in the boy's death.

Mandela was openly supportive of his wife and believed the charges were part of the government's efforts to harass and discredit himself and Winnie. Winnie Mandela was eventually convicted for her purported role in the murder and she received a light jail sentence which was overturned upon appeal. To show his allegiance and belief in his wife's innocence, Mandela attended each day of the trial and appeal. However, in April 1992, Mandela publicly announced his separation from Winnie Mandela after thirty-three years of marriage, citing personal difficulties. Many have speculated that it

was not her alleged criminal activities that caused the rift but a love affair Winnie had started while Mandela was in prison and continued to pursue after his release.

CODESA

During the months that his wife was on trial, Mandela also had to deal with political tensions in his negotiations with de Klerk. Although the trust between the two men had been permanently damaged by de Klerk's inaction in dealing with violence against the ANC, Mandela nonetheless continued to progress in his negotiations. Negotiations shifted in July 1991 when Mandela was elected president of the ANC. Among his first acts in office he successfully organized a meeting between the government and nineteen opposition groups, the Convention for a Democratic South Africa (CODESA), at the World Trade Center near Johannesburg's airport. The conference had one purpose: to create a new constitution that would provide universal adult suffrage and include a bill of rights providing civil and political rights for all races, an independent judiciary, and the elimination of the homeland governments and the reincorporation of their territories. In his opening speech, Mandela noted the importance of the occasion:

> The challenge which Codesa places before each one of us is to unshackle ourselves from the past and build

Winnie's Downfall

In 1985, during her husband's twenty-first year of imprisonment, Winnie Mandela returned to Orlando after eight years of banishment in Brandfort. In the late 1980s she became an increasingly controversial figure, causing antiapartheid activists, including members of the ANC, to distance themselves from her. In 1988, as African-on-African violence increased, she alienated many of her supporters by endorsing "necklacing" killings in which tires filled with gasoline were placed around a victim's neck and set on fire. Further, she acquired a group of bodyguards, young men, many of them with criminal associations, who jokingly called themselves the Mandela United Football Club. In December 1988 her bodyguards abducted, tortured, and beat four black men in Winnie Mandela's home, allegedly in her presence. One of the men was killed and his body was discovered on January 6, 1989; one of the bodyguards was found guilty of the murder in 1989. In July 1990 Winnie was arrested and charged with kidnapping and assault in relation to the crime; she was found guilty in May 1991. Sentenced to six years in prison, she appealed the verdict.

Despite Mandela's public support for his wife during her legal battle, the couple's marriage was in serious trouble due to Winnie's years-long affair with another man. Humiliated and angry, Mandela moved out in 1992, announcing his separation in a public statement. The couple later divorced in 1996.

anew. Codesa can be the beginning of reconstruction. Let our common commitment to the future of our country inspire us to build a South Africa of which we can be truly proud.[62]

Stalemate and Violence

Despite good intentions by the delegates, the talks were plagued by problems over achieving a constitution that would provide a balance of power among the races but also satisfy the government as well as the other delegates. The white minority government was not ready to give up its disproportional representation, and the talks stalled in June 1992.

Later that month, violence erupted again when two hundred Zulus attacked a settlement in Boipatong, located on the southern outskirts of Johannesburg, killing forty-six Africans, mostly women and children. Again, police involvement and inaction was apparent, and the ANC formally broke off negotiations.

De Klerk and Mandela shake hands during a meeting of the Convention for a Democratic South Africa (CODESA). These meetings helped bring about the collapse of apartheid.

In further protest, the ANC organized a national strike over two days in August 1992. The strike was an enormous success, with more than 4 million people participating. Addressing a crowd of one hundred thousand in front of central government buildings in Pretoria, Mandela called upon the government to show its support for democracy in its actions: "We are here to take South Africa along the road to peace and democracy. . . . All the people of our country await the response of the government."[63]

Election

Despite the public halt to negotiations, Mandela continued to meet with de Klerk secretly. In September 1992, after a few weeks of private talks, Mandela and de Klerk jointly issued a document titled the Record of Understanding, calling for the resumption of negotiations. In May 1993 CODESA talks resumed.

Chief Buthelezi reacted angrily to the resumed talks. Although Mandela and de Klerk tried to bring Buthelezi into their negotiations, he refused, instead forging an alliance with several extreme right-wing groups such as the Conservative Party—largely formed by racist whites who had left the National Party due to de Klerk's reforms.

Nonetheless, Mandela led the ANC and the National Party to negotiate a timetable for the creation of a new constitution and the first multiracial election in the country's history. Elections would take place in April 1994.

The key to the success of the negotiations was a policy of limited-time power sharing, an idea sponsored by Mandela's old friend and Communist Party member Joe Slovo. For a limited term, governmental power would be shared by the National Party, the ANC, and other political organizations until the April elections. This assured de Klerk's Nationalist Party that in giving up its minority power rule it would not be left out of the new government. This multiparty administration, called the Transitional Executive Council, took power in December 1993.

President Mandela

The national election was held over four days in April, and the results were no surprise to anyone involved. The ANC received 62.7 percent of the vote, and as leader of the party, Nelson Mandela won the seat as the first black president in South African history.

On May 10, 1994, Mandela took the oath of office. In his inauguration speech he celebrated not only the victory of the new government but also the end of oppression: "Out of the experience of an extraordinary human disaster that lasted too long, must be born a society of which all humanity will be proud. . . . Never, never and never again shall it be that this beautiful land will again experience the oppression of one by another."[64]

Inherited Troubles

The celebrations did not last long, however, as Mandela and his administration were immediately faced with the seemingly insurmountable task of undoing three centuries of racist government. In 1994 South Africa contained approximately 50 million people, of which 6 million were unemployed, 9 million were without homes, 10 million were without access to running water, and 23 million were without electricity. Among blacks, illiteracy was over 60 percent and the infant mortality rate was 80 deaths per 1,000 people. Further, as historian Leonard Friedman writes, all levels of government and private industry in South Africa were steeped in institutionalized racism:

South Africa was racked by the cumulative effects of slavery, conquest, colonialism, segregation, apartheid, and urbanization. The judiciary, the bureaucracy, the army, the police force, the municipal

"Let a New Age Dawn"

Soon after Mandela and de Klerk came to an agreement on a peaceful transfer of power to a democratically elected government, the two men were jointly awarded the Nobel Peace Prize on December 10, 1993, in Oslo, Norway. The following is an excerpt of Mandela's acceptance speech, reprinted from the ANC website.

We stand here today as nothing more than a representative of the millions of our people who dared to rise up against a social system whose very essence is war, violence, racism, oppression, repression and the impoverishment of an entire people....

Because of their courage and persistence for many years, we can, today, even set the dates when all humanity will join together to celebrate one of the outstanding human victories of our century....

When that moment comes, we shall, together, rejoice in a common victory over racism, apartheid and white minority rule....

Such a society should never allow again that there should be prisoners of conscience nor that any person's human rights should be violated.

Neither should it ever happen that once more the avenues to peaceful change are blocked by usurpers who seek to take power away from the people, in pursuit of their own, ignoble purposes....

But there are still some within our country who wrongly believe they can make a contribution to the cause of justice and peace by clinging to the shibboleths [catchwords identified with a group or cause] that have been proved to spell nothing but disaster.

It remains our hope that these, too, will be blessed with sufficient reason to realise that history will not be denied and that the new society cannot be created by reproducing the repugnant past, however refined or enticingly repackaged....

Let it never be said by future generations that indifference, cynicism or selfishness made us fail to live up to the ideals of humanism which the Nobel Peace Prize encapsulates.

Let a new age dawn!

Mandela and de Klerk accept the Nobel Peace Prize in Oslo in 1992.

administrations, and the media were all dominated by white men who had been brought up in a racist milieu and trained to serve the apartheid state.[65]

Numerous factors threatened to undermine the new democracy: violence and crime, the refusal of people to pay their rents or service fees, white racists conspiring to damage the new government, and a persistent economic slump. Mandela had been brought to office by millions who had high expectations of his presidency, and Mandela was immediately pressured to fulfill them. However, the country did not have enough money or qualified educated blacks, which made it impossible to make anything but slow progress in his reforms.

Slow Change

Mandela insisted upon patience from his constituents, saying, "The government literally does not have the money to meet the demands that are being advanced. . . . We must rid ourselves of the culture of entitlement that the government must promptly deliver whatever is that we demand."[66]

To raise money for his reforms, Mandela embarked on international fund-raising missions all over the globe. He traveled around Africa, Europe, and the United States describing the turmoil and dire need his country was experiencing and the hope he

had for change. In one speech in London, Mandela said:

> The poverty, decay in the social fabric, and profound inequality that are the product of the past, can only be eradicated with your co-operation. Thus, we can build a truly non-racial and non-sexist society and ensure that our achievements in the political transition become more than formal declarations in constitutional and legal documents.[67]

While response was good, it was far from adequate. Few countries or private investors were eager to invest money in the unstable and violent country.

Although Mandela remained optimistic and pointed to the slow, positive change his administration had created in its first year, many people saw it as a time of planning rather than achievement. As Friedman writes, it was "a time when most black South Africans experienced no improvement in the quality of their lives."[68]

However, despite hard times and criticism, Mandela's government was internationally recognized for its achievements. In a *Business Day* article, one reporter said that "there can be no doubt that President Mandela's government is the best in South Africa's troubled history."[69]

Uniting the Country

Understanding the new government had created fear and anxiety among the white population, Mandela made numerous efforts to unite the country. He continually repeated that whites had as much a place in the new South Africa as everyone else. During his administration he made such great efforts to appease and assure whites that he received criticism from his black constituency that he was not doing enough for them.

The climax of Mandela's efforts to unite the races happened during the 1995 Rugby World Cup tournament that was hosted by South Africa. It was the largest sporting event in the country's history and was of significant symbolic importance. During apartheid, South Africa had been expelled from the World Cup tournament. Further, blacks had long ignored the sport because it was dominated by the Boers. During the 1995 World Cup, Mandela publicly supported the team and made friends with the captain, who taught the team to sing the words of the ANC anthem, "Nkosi Sikelel iAfrika" which they sang at games. Mandela's efforts turned the tournament into a multiracial event, and when the South African team won the tournament, the entire country, both black and white, celebrated together.

Setting an Example

Despite his unification efforts, Mandela's presidency was far from smooth.

Government officials of all races abused their posts. One of the key figures in corruption in his government was his estranged wife Winnie Mandela, whom he had hired as a minister out of a sense of allegiance and duty to her. However, Winnie abused her office; in 1996 Mandela was forced to fire her when she spoke out against his leadership. Immediately afterward, he sued for and was granted a divorce.

Mandela himself seemed unassailable in his behavior. After years in prison, he was used to an austere lifestyle. Unlike his predecessors, as president he lived frugally and hoped to set an example for the new South African government. Although he earned a large annual salary, he donated a third of it to the ANC and the Nelson Mandela Children's Fund, a charity to aid the country's overwhelming population of poor youth. Further, he donated to charity the large royalties from his memoirs and the money awarded to him for the Nobel Peace Prize.

Retirement

From the beginning of his presidency, Mandela had no intention of seeking reelection, although he was assured of a clean victory despite his administration's troubles. He thought that a new South Africa should be passed on to a younger generation to revitalize and reinvigorate it. At the end of his term in 1999, he turned the leadership of

President Mandela greets the world champion South African rugby team in 1995. The tournament was the first multiracial sporting event after the end of apartheid.

the party over to his deputy president, Thabo Mbeki, the son of Govan Mbeki, one of his fellow Rivonia Trial defendants.

At the end of his presidency Mandela looked forward to many of the simple pleasures his lifelong commitment to the struggle had denied him, such as spending time with his children and grandchildren. Additionally, he married for a third time in 1998; his bride, Graca Machel, is the widow of former Mozambique president Samora Machel. The two plan to spend more time together, dividing their stays between Mandela's house in

his ancestral Umtata and Machel's Mozambique mansion.

However, Mandela's retirement is far from inactive. After spending twenty-seven years of his life in prison, he feels he has much lost time to make up for and has expressed his need to remain useful. Mandela concedes, "I have retired, but if there's anything in the world that would kill me it is to wake up in the morning and not know what to do."[70]

Fortunately, there is always plenty of work for him to do. As South Africa's most beloved and respected statesman, Mandela remains active although unofficially engaged in politics. His calendar is filled with meetings with world leaders all over the globe. His talent for mediating conflicts has been put to use in negotiating peace in political disputes in the Congo and Burundi.

Mandela remains an outspoken figure, ready to attack injustice wherever he sees it around the world. His opinions have not always been popular with powerful world leaders. For instance, in 2002 and 2003 Mandela openly criticized the administrations of both George W. Bush and Tony Blair for invading Iraq after his offer to mediate between Iraq and the Western countries went unanswered by the Bush administration. Additionally, at home, he has been critical of numerous policies of his own successor, Thabo Mbeki.

Mandela has also been actively championing important causes, particularly education for black South Africans and the fight against the African AIDS epidemic. When he was not crisscrossing the globe, he also worked on a second volume of his memoirs, which deals with his years in office. In his research for the book, he frequently called on people involved, including old opponents like F.W. de Klerk.

Mandela unveils a monument to his life's work at his birthplace in Mvezo in 2000. He remains a hero and idol to people of all races around the world.

Legacy

In July 2003 Mandela celebrated his eighty-fifth birthday at a star-studded party in Johannesburg attended by more than sixteen hundred celebrities, leaders, and friends. Although Mandela was diagnosed with prostate cancer in 2001, after treatment the condition appears to be in remission and his health has remained robust.

Nonetheless, many in South Africa and the ANC look to the post-Mandela future with a mixture of anticipation and fear. Although many in the ANC want to see the organization shift away from the conciliation and appeasement of whites, which characterized the Mandela era, many wonder what will happen to the government and the country without his considerable symbolic presence in South Africa. Meanwhile, Mandela has made his own plans. He muses, "In

heaven, I will be looking for the nearest branch of the ANC."[71]

Mandela was and remains not only a key leader, negotiator, and peacemaker but also a figure of great importance and strength to a great number of South African people of all races. His life story of commitment and struggle in the face of poverty, danger, and imprisonment spans more than eight decades and has become almost a national legend.

Through sacrifice, courage, persistence, and diplomacy, Mandela sought after and attained in his country what no leader—white or black—before him had: peaceful and productive coexistence among the races. Although troubles continue to befall South Africa, because of Mandela's efforts and those of his colleagues and followers, all of its citizens have the right and responsibility for shaping its future.

Notes

Introduction: Father of the New South Africa

1. Nelson Mandela, *Long Walk to Freedom: The Autobiography of Nelson Mandela.* New York: Little, Brown, 1994, p. 83.

Chapter 1: Early Lessons

2. Nelson Mandela Foundation, "Nelson Mandela Biography." www.nelsonmandela.org.
3. Mandela, *Long Walk to Freedom,* p. 19.
4. Fatima Meer, *Higher than Hope: The Authorized Biography of Nelson Mandela.* New York: Harper & Row, 1988, p. 14.
5. Martin Meredith, *Nelson Mandela.* New York: Thomas Dunne, 1998, p. 19.
6. Mandela, *Long Walk to Freedom,* p. 45.
7. Meredith, *Nelson Mandela,* p. 26.

Chapter 2: A Political Awakening

8. Mandela, *Long Walk to Freedom,* p. 58.
9. Quoted in Meredith, *Nelson Mandela,* p. 33.
10. Mandela, *Long Walk to Freedom,* p. 60.
11. Mandela, *Long Walk to Freedom,* p. 61.

12. Quoted in Meer, *Higher than Hope,* p. 26.
13. Mary Benson, *Nelson Mandela: The Man and the Movement.* New York: W.W. Norton, 1986, p. 31.
14. Mandela, *Long Walk to Freedom,* p. 74.
15. Mandela, *Long Walk to Freedom,* p. 75.
16. Mandela, *Long Walk to Freedom,* p. 83.
17. Quoted in Meredith, *Nelson Mandela,* p. 46.
18. Mandela, *Long Walk to Freedom,* p. 85.
19. Quoted in Nelson Mandela, *The Struggle Is My Life.* New York: Pathfinder, 1990, p. 19.

Chapter 3: Learning to Lead

20. Quoted in Meer, *Higher than Hope,* pp. 39–40.
21. Quoted in Meredith, *Nelson Mandela,* p. 52.
22. Benson, *Nelson Mandela,* p. 30.
23. Quoted in Meredith, *Nelson Mandela,* p. 66.
24. Mandela, *Long Walk to Freedom,* p. 97.
25. Mandela, *Long Walk to Freedom,* p. 100.
26. Mandela, *The Struggle Is My Life,* p. 31.
27. Meer, *Higher than Hope,* p. 58.

Chapter 4: Freedom Fighter

28. Quoted in Benson, *Nelson Mandela*, p. 68.
29. Mandela, *Long Walk to Freedom*, p. 186.
30. Quoted in Tony Pinchuck, *Introducing Mandela*. Cambridge, UK: Totem Books, 1994, p. 90.
31. Mandela, *Long Walk to Freedom*, p. 233.
32. Meer, *Higher than Hope*, p. 151.

Chapter 5: Revolutionary

33. Mandela, *Long Walk to Freedom*, p. 232.
34. Quoted in Benson, *Nelson Mandela*, p. 104.
35. Quoted in Benson, *Nelson Mandela*, p. 104.
36. Mandela, *Long Walk to Freedom*, p. 239.
37. Quoted in Meer, *Higher than Hope*, p. 164.
38. Nelson Mandela, *Mandela: An Illustrated Biography*. New York: Little, Brown, 1996, p. 91.
39. Mandela, *Mandela*, p. 91.
40. Quoted in Africa Within, "Black Man in a White Court: Nelson Mandela's First Court Statement—1962." www.africawithin.com.
41. Quoted in Meredith, *Nelson Mandela*, p. 214.
42. Nelson Mandela, *I Am Prepared to Die*. London: International Defence and Aid Fund for Southern Africa, 1984, p. 1.
43. Mandela, *I Am Prepared to Die*, p. 26.
44. Mandela, *Long Walk to Freedom*, p. 314.
45. Mandela, *I Am Prepared to Die*, p. 33.
46. Mandela, *I Am Prepared to Die*, p. 36.

Chapter 6: Prisoner of Conscience

47. Mandela, *Long Walk to Freedom*, p. 338.
48. Mandela, *Long Walk to Freedom*, pp. 340–41.
49. Mandela, *Long Walk to Freedom*, p. 351.
50. Quoted in Meer, *Higher than Hope*, p. 269.
51. Mandela, *Long Walk to Freedom*, p. 389.
52. Mandela, *The Struggle Is My Life*, pp. 190–92.
53. Meer, *Higher than Hope*, p. 313.
54. Quoted in Meredith, *Nelson Mandela*, p. 335.
55. Mandela, *The Struggle Is My Life*, pp. 194–96.
56. Mandela, *Long Walk to Freedom*, pp. 466–67.
57. Mandela, *Long Walk to Freedom*, p. 485.

Chapter 7: Statesman

58. Nelson Mandela, *Nelson Mandela speaks: forging a Democratic, nonracial South Africa*, ed. Steve Clark. New York: Pathfinder, 1993, pp. 24–28.
59. Nelson Mandela, "Address to the Joint Session of the Houses of

Congress of the U.S.A., Washington, D.C., June 26, 1990," African National Congress. www.anc.org.za.

60. Quoted in Meredith, *Nelson Mandela*, p. 426.
61. Meredith, *Nelson Mandela*, p. 432.
62. Mandela, *Nelson Mandela Speaks*, pp. 148–52.
63. Mandela, *Nelson Mandela, Speaks*, p. 167.
64. Quoted in Nelson Mandela, "Statement of the President of the African National Congress Nelson Rolihlahla Mandela at His Inauguration as President of the Democratic Republic of South Africa, Union Buildings, Pretoria, 10 May 1994." African National Congress. www.anc.org.za.
65. Leonard Friedman, *A History of South Africa*, rev. ed. New Haven, CT: Yale University Press, 1995, p. 256.
66. Quoted in Meredith, *Nelson Mandela*, p. 526.
67. Quoted in Nelson Mandela, "Address by Mandela to the CBI Conference, London, 10 July 1996." African National Congress. www.anc.org.za.
68. Friedman, *A History of South Africa*, p. 267.
69. Quoted in Friedman, *A History of South Africa*, p. 267.
70. Quoted in Anthony Sampson, "Mandela at 85," *Observer (UK)*, July 6, 2003.
71. Quoted in Sampson, "Mandela at 85."

CHRONOLOGY

1918
Rolihlahla "Nelson" Mandela is born on July 18 in Qunu, South Africa.

1941
Mandela arrives in Johannesburg.

1944
Mandela joins the African National Congress (ANC); he marries Evelyn Ntoko Mase.

1948
The Afrikaner Nationalist Party comes to power; apartheid policies begin.

1950
Mandela is elected president of the ANC Youth League.

1952
Mandela orchestrates the Defiance Campaign.

1955
The Congress of the People adopts the Freedom Charter on June 25–26.

1956
On December 5, Mandela is arrested with 155 others on grounds of high treason.

1957
Nelson and Evelyn Mandela divorce; Mandela meets Nomzamo "Winnie" Madikizela.

1958
Mandela and Madikizela marry.

1960
In March sixty-nine Africans are killed by police officers in the Sharpesville Massacre; a state of emergency is declared; the ANC is banned.

1961
Mandela and the remaining treason trial defendants are acquitted and released in March; Mandela goes underground. Umkhonto we Sizwe (MK) conducts its first sabotage attacks in December.

1962
Mandela is caught, tried for inciting a strike and leaving the country illegally, and is sentenced to five years of hard labor.

1963
The Rivonia Trial begins.

1964

Mandela and Rivonia Trial codefendants are sentenced to life in prison on Robben Island.

1976

Riots occur throughout South Africa in response to the massacre of schoolchildren in Soweto.

1982

Mandela is transferred to the Pollsmoor prison in Cape Town.

1988

Mandela is transferred to Victor Verster Prison.

1989

F.W. de Klerk becomes prime minister.

1990

De Klerk ends the ban on the ANC and other apartheid groups; Mandela is freed on February 11; the ANC begins negotiations with the government.

1991

Multiparty CODESA negotiations begin.

1994

The first multiracial democratic elections are held in South Africa in April; Mandela is inaugurated as the first black president of South Africa in May.

1996

Nelson and Winnie Mandela divorce.

1998

Mandela marries Graca Machel.

1999

Mandela retires from the presidency without seeking a second term.

2003

A national celebration is held in honor of Mandela's eighty-fifth birthday on July 18.

FOR FURTHER READING

Books

Nelson Mandela, *The Words of Nelson Mandela*. Ed. Jennifer Crwys-Williams. Seacaucus, NJ: Birch Lane, 1998. A collection of quotes by Nelson Mandela organized by subject. Although some of the quotes have notation to provide context, most are without source or context information.

Nelson Mandela and Fidel Castro, *How Far We Slaves Have Come! South Africa and Cuba in Today's World*. New York: Pathfinder, 1991. A collection of three essays by Mandela and Castro on the status of the South African and Cuban revolts. It includes a chronology and brief biographies of both leaders.

Steven Otfinoski, *Nelson Mandela: The Fight Against Apartheid*. Brookfield, CT: Millbrook, 1992. Written for young adults, this biography provides a succinct outline of Mandela's life from birth to the eve of his presidency.

Tony Pinchuck, *Introducing Mandela*. Cambridge, UK: Totem Books, 1994. This easy-to-read, illustrated graphic biography covers Mandela's life up to his presidency.

Websites

South Africa Info (www.safrica.info). This useful and photo-rich site provides a brief biography of Nelson Mandela with numerous hyperlinks to articles and historic documents for cross-referencing. The site also includes links to selected speeches and articles on Mandela.

The Story of Africa, BBC World Service (www.bbc.co.uk/worldservice/africa/features/storyofafrica). This website tells the history of the African continent and cultures using text, photos, and audio and video clips. It includes numerous time lines and suggestions for further reading.

Videos

Mandela and De Klerk. VHS. Hallmark Entertainment and Bernard Sofronski Productions, 1997. This biographical film relates the story of Nelson Mandela (played by Sidney Poitier) from his years as a revolutionary against F.W. de Klerk's (played by Michael Caine) government and incarceration to his election as a South African president.

Mandela: Son of Africa, Father of a Nation. VHS. Produced by Jonathan Demme. Ryko Distributions, 1997. This 1997 film, nominated for the Academy Award for Best Documentary, follows Nelson Mandela from his early days and tribal education through his work with the African National Congress to his election as Africa's first black president.

Works Consulted

Books

Mary Benson, *Nelson Mandela: The Man and the Movement.* New York: W.W. Norton, 1986. Written by a longtime friend of Nelson Mandela, this biography chronicles Mandela's life up until the mid-1980s, when he was still imprisoned on Robben Island and South Africa was suffering through some of its most violent years. Much of the biography involves the lives of Mandela's second wife, Winnie Mandela, and their children and the efforts to free Mandela from prison.

Leonard Friedman, *A History of South Africa.* Rev. ed. New Haven, CT: Yale University Press, 1995. This book provides a detailed history of the nation of South Africa before and after European colonization, up through 1995, the first year of Mandela's presidency. It includes a chronology, numerous illustrations, and an appendix of statistics on the country.

Nelson Mandela, *I Am Prepared to Die.* London: International Defence and Aid Fund for Southern Africa, 1984. Published while Mandela was imprisoned on Robben Island, this collection provides excerpts of court transcripts from the 1962 and 1963–1964 trials against Mandela, including the titular speech made as part of his testimony during the so-called Rivonia trial.

———, *Long Walk to Freedom: The Autobiography of Nelson Mandela.* New York: Little, Brown, 1994. This autobiography, much of it written during the mid-1970s while he was imprisoned on Robben Island, covers Mandela's life up to 1994 in great detail. It is the seminal text on which most other biographies on Mandela have been based. Few black-and-white photographs accompany the text.

———, *Mandela: An Illustrated Biography.* New York: Little, Brown, 1996. Adapted from his autobiography, *Long Walk to Freedom*, this illustrated version covers Mandela's life from his country childhood to the eve of his presidency as the first black president of South Africa. Many photos in color and black and white accompany the text.

————, *Nelson Mandela speaks: forging a Democratic, nonracial South Africa.* Ed. Steve Clark. New York: Pathfinder, 1993. This collection of speeches covers the period from Mandela's release from prison to his campaign for presidency. Also includes a brief biographical note and a chronology of events from 1990 through 1993.

————, *Nelson Mandela Speeches, 1990: Intensify the Struggle to Abolish Apartheid.* Ed. Greg McCartan. New York: Pathfinder, 1990. This collection of letters and speeches covers July 1989 through May 1990, including correspondence from Mandela to Prime Ministers Botha and de Klerk as well as speeches given following his release from prison.

————, *The Struggle Is My Life.* New York: Pathfinder, 1990. This collection of speeches, writings, documents, and interviews covers the period of Mandela's first involvement with the ANC to his release from prison in 1990. It includes a few black-and-white stock photographs.

Fatima Meer, *Higher than Hope: The Authorized Biography of Nelson Mandela.* New York: Harper & Row, 1988. Released two years before Mandela was released from Victor Verster Prison, this biography draws on numerous interviews with Mandela's friends and family and includes an appendix of letters written by Mandela.

Martin Meredith, *Nelson Mandela.* New York: Thomas Dunne, 1998. This unbiased and well-researched biography covers Mandela's life from birth to his retirement from the presidency. It includes an extensive bibliography that offers source references for further research.

Periodical

Anthony Sampson, "Mandela at 85," *Observer (UK),* July 6, 2003.

Internet Sources

Africa Within, "Black Man in a White Court: Nelson Mandela's First Court Statement—1962." www.africawith in.com.

Nelson Mandela, "Acceptance Speech of the President of the African National Congress, Nelson Mandela, at the Nobel Peace Prize Award Ceremony," African National Congress. www.anc.org.za.

————, "Address by Mandela to the CBI Conference, London, 10 July 1996," African National Congress. www.anc.org.za.

————, "Address to the Joint Session of the Houses of Congress of the U.S.A., Washington, D.C., June 26, 1990," African National Congress. www.anc.org.za.

————, "The Freedom Charter," African National Congress. www. anc. org.za.

————, "A New Menace in Africa," African National Congress. www. anc.org.za.

———, "Statement of the President of the African National Congress Nelson Rolihlahla Mandela at His Inauguration as President of the Democratic Republic of South Africa, Union Buildings, Pretoria, 10 May 1994," African National Congress. www.anc.org.za.

Nelson Mandela Foundation, "Nelson Mandela Biography." www.nelson mandela.org.

Website

African National Congress (www.anc.org.za). This website provides an extensive collection of Mandela's speeches from the 1950s to the present. It also includes resources such as historical documents relevant to the antiapartheid movement and biographies of key figures, including Mandela, Oliver Tambo, and Walter Sisulu.

INDEX

PICTURE CREDITS

ABOUT THE AUTHOR

Andy Koopmans is the author of several books, including biographies of Bruce Lee, Charles Lindbergh, Madonna, and the Osbournes. His other nonfiction work includes *Leopold and Loeb: Teen Killers, Understanding Great Literature: Lord of the Flies, Examining Popular Culture: Crimes and Criminals,* and *Discovering Rwanda.* He is also a fiction writer, essayist, and poet. He lives in Seattle, Washington, with his wife, Angela Mihm, and their pets, Bubz, Licorice, and Zachary. He wishes to thank his wife, Angela, and the staff at Lucent Books, particularly his editor, Jennifer Skancke, for their assistance with this manuscript.